Love Sayings

wit & wisdom
of romance, courtship,
& marriage

By Bradford G. Wheler

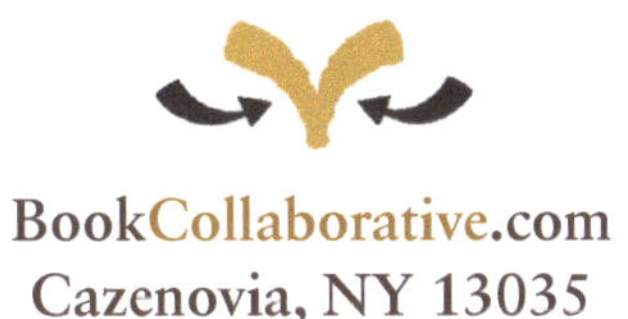

BookCollaborative.com
Cazenovia, NY 13035

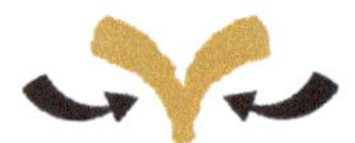

BookCollaborative.com
PO Box 403
Cazenovia, NY 13035

BookCollaborative.com@gmail.com

ISBN-13: 978-0-9822538-8-5

Love, Quotations, Art, Humor & Wit

PRINTED IN THE UNITED STATES OF AMERICA

US Retail Price $24.95

Design by Lorie DeWorken, MINDtheMARGINS, LLC

Table of Contents

Introduction

I would like to thank everyone who participated in this project. In particular, I wanted to thank the artists and photographers who contributed their original works to this book.

It was exciting to check my email and find a wonderful range of new submissions from a wide variety of artists and photographers. The book features 48 artists from 14 different countries. Many of the artists in this book are full-time professional artists or photographers. Others love painting and photographing as a hobby. They exhibit a wonderful range of artistic styles.

I established BookCollaborative.com to publish books based on the content provided by artists. The goal is to create a collaborative community to promote art in general. At the same time, artists have the opportunity to promote their own artwork in books. I also want it to be interesting and fun. For more information go to www.BookCollaborative.com.

In selecting images for LOVE SAYINGS, I tried to be inclusive. However, some artwork simply didn't fit the theme of this book. Other artwork did not make the cut due to various factors, such as missing the deadline, low image resolution, etc.

Printing premium quality color books with Lightning Source

Inc.'s on-demand system is about six times as expensive as printing black-and-white books. This factor limits the page count of a reasonably priced color book. It my hope that as technology progresses, the price for color on-demand printing will come down. This would allow greater flexibility in the size of color books as well as the number of pages.

This book would not have been possible without the help of many others. They include Lorie DeWorken of MINDtheMARGINS for professional page design and layout, Marcia Abramson for her proofreading and editing, and Brian Hoke of Bentley Hoke Consulting who helped with all things web related. I would like to thank my lovely wife, Julie, for her support on this project and everything else.

I'm sure this book includes errors. For those I apologize.

Most of all I hope people enjoy *LOVE SAYINGS: wit and wisdom of romance, courtship, & marriage*.

Bradford G. Wheler
Fort Pierce, FL & Cazenovia, NY
March 2015

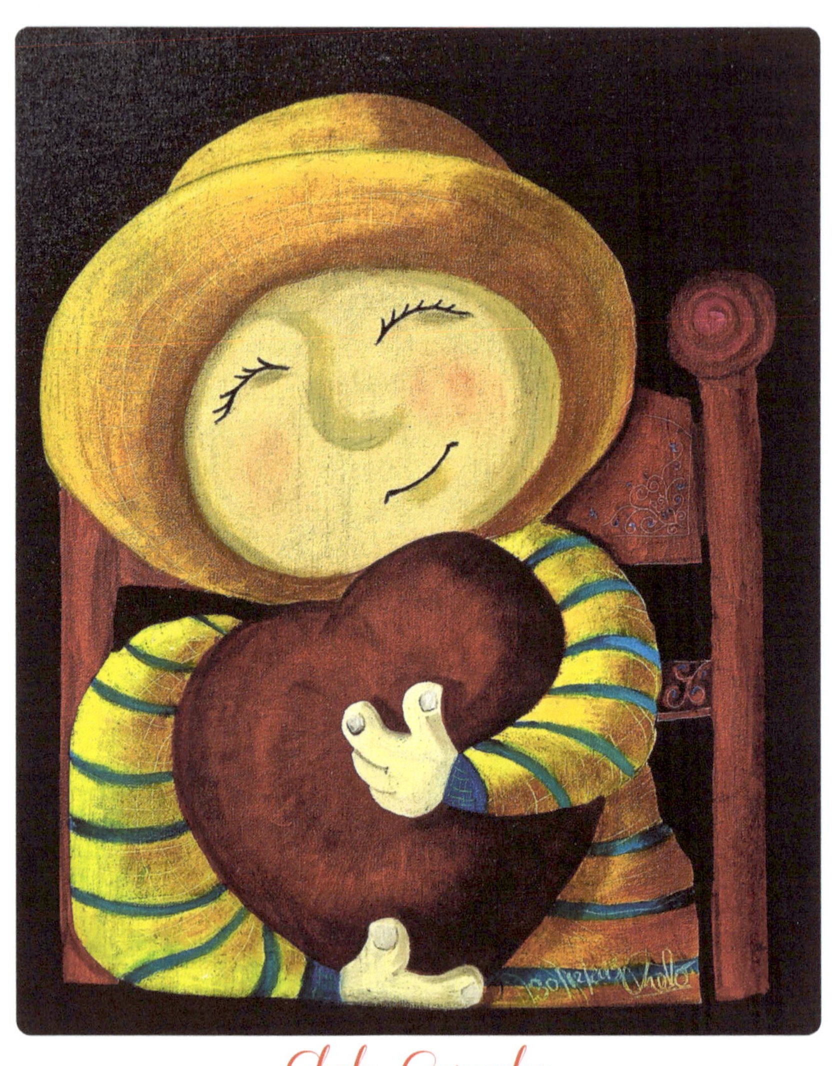

Chelo Gonzalez

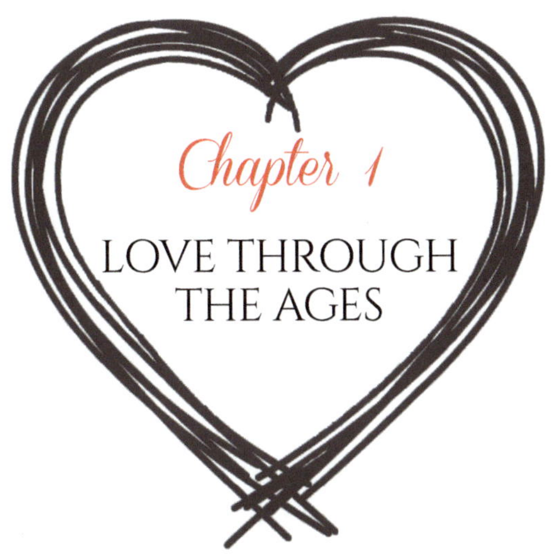

Chapter 1

LOVE THROUGH THE AGES

Kind words can be short and easy to speak,
but their echoes are truly endless.

- MOTHER TERESA (1910 – 1997)

Love is a game that two
can play and both win.

- EVA GABOR (1919 – 1995)

I don't think anyone knows I love the girl;
I haven't done anything really silly yet.

-TITUS MACCIUS PLAUTUS (255 – 184 BC)

Love is an irresistible desire
to be irresistibly desired.

- ROBERT FROST (1874 – 1963)

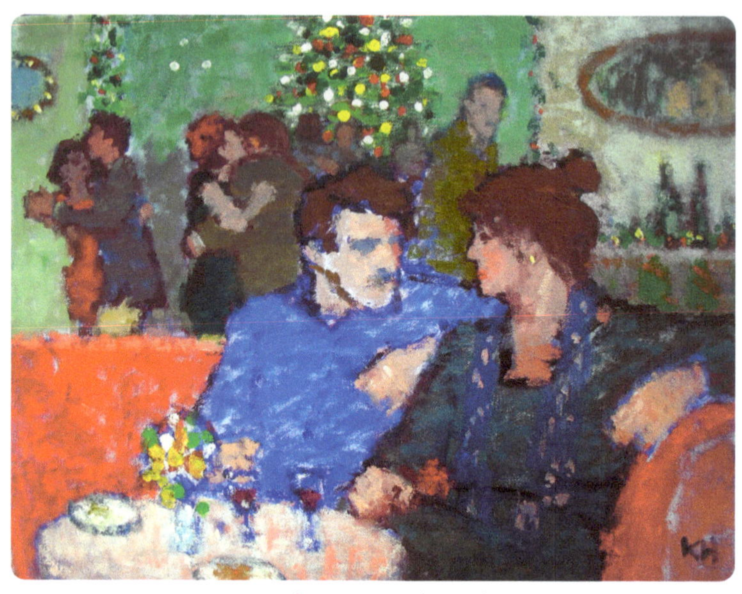

Kate Huntington

A fellow who sets out on love's road with an empty purse is taking on greater labors than Hercules.

- TITUS MACCIUS PLAUTUS (255 – 184 BC)

The gods never let us love and be wise at the same time.

- PUBLILIUS SYRUS (85 – 43 BC)

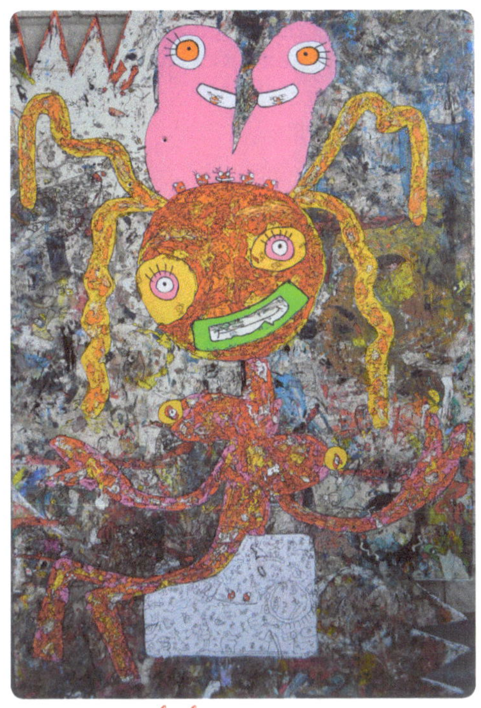

Vhilo Persson

One is very crazy when in love.

-SIGMUND FREUD (1856 – 1939)

Love is a serious mental disease.

-PLATO (424/423 – 348/347 BC)

Love takes up where knowledge leaves off.

- THOMAS AQUINAS (1225 – 1274)

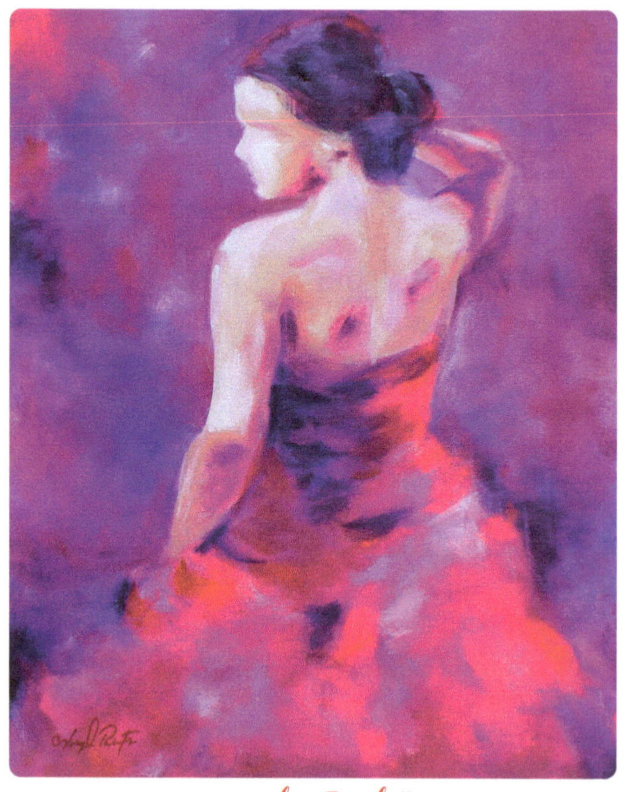

Joseph Palotas

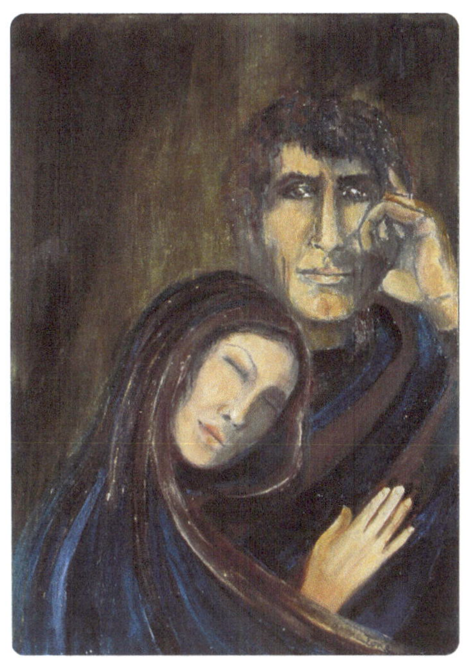

Ione Citrin

Every man who will not have softening of
the heart must at last have softening of the brain.

- G.K. CHESTERTON (1874 – 1936)

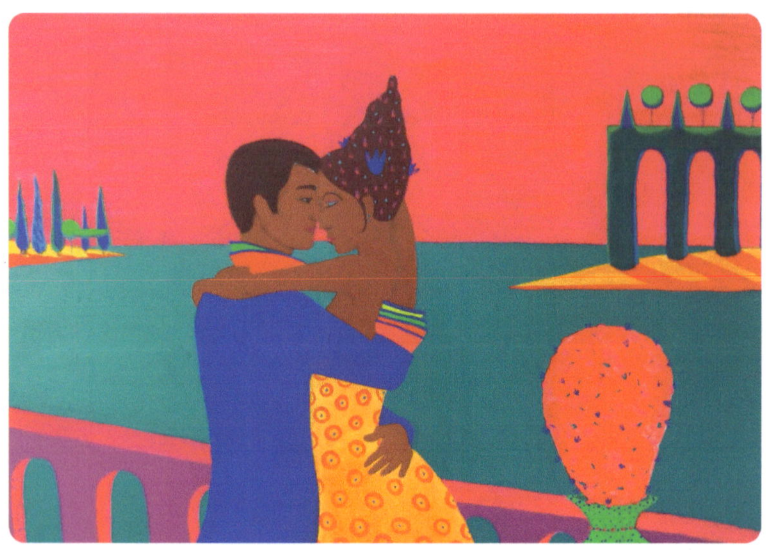

Katrina Avotina

When two people love each other, they don't look at each other, they look in the same direction.

- GINGER ROGERS (1911 – 1995)

Great loves too must be endured.

- COCO CHANEL (1883 – 1971)

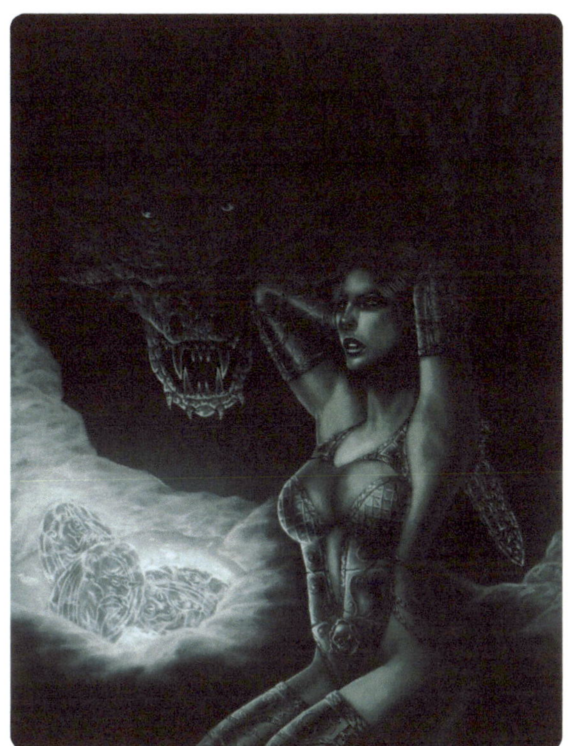

Kayla Ascencio

Love is the crocodile on the river of desire.

- BHARTRIHARI (6TH OR 7TH CENTURY)

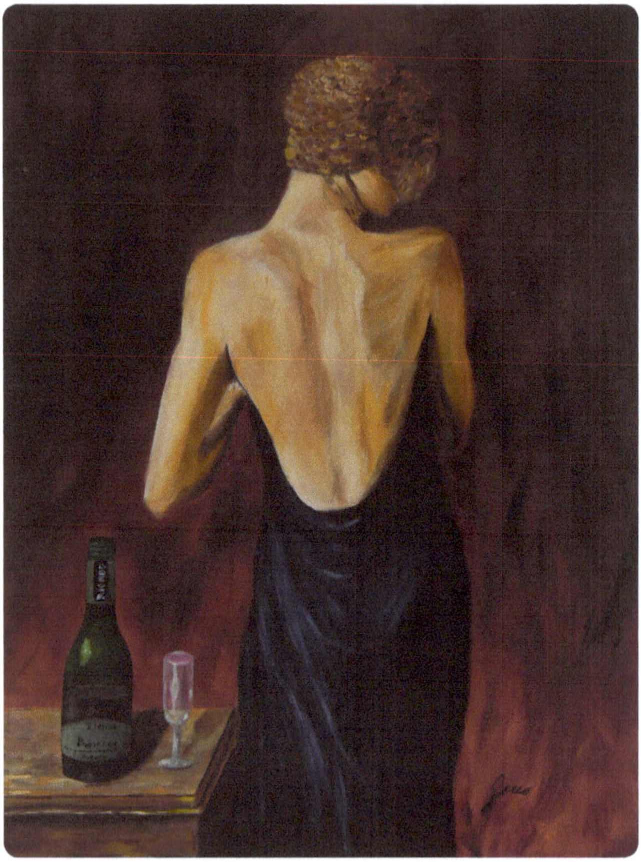

Gino Di Dio

A woman loves you or she hates you; there's no other choice.

- PUBLILIUS SYRUS (85 – 43 BC)

Never forget that the most powerful force on earth is love.

- NELSON ROCKEFELLER (1908 – 1979)

Love is the greatest refreshment in life.

- PABLO PICASSO (1881 – 1973)

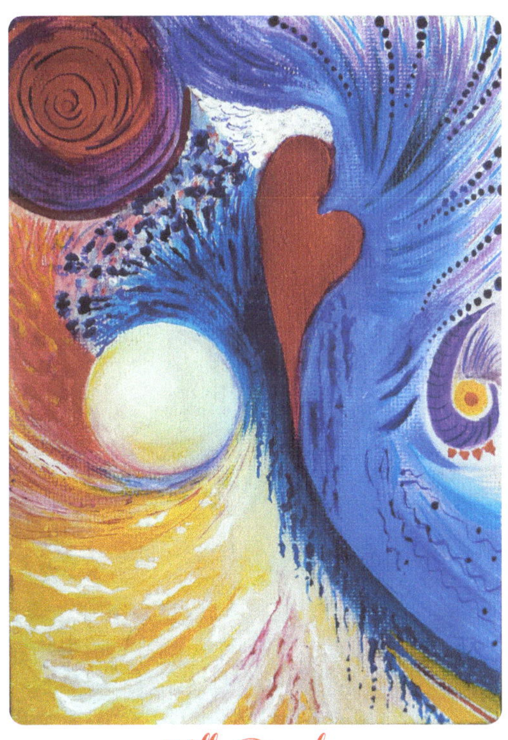

Jill Ryals

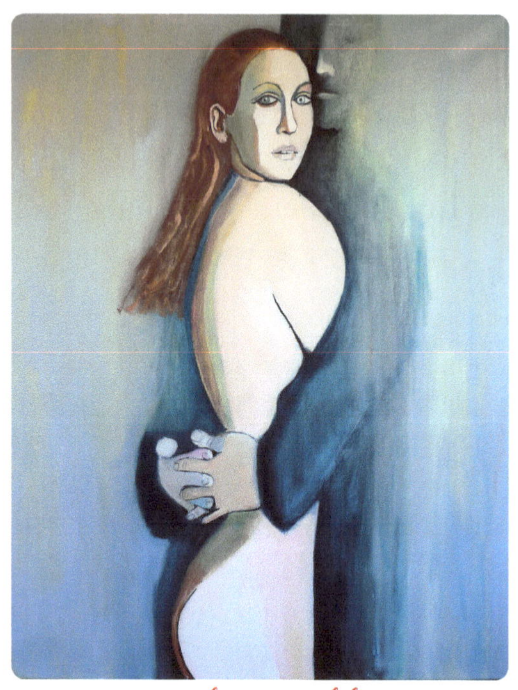

Carolyn Schlam

Being deeply loved by someone gives you strength, while loving someone deeply gives you courage.

- LAO TZU (6TH CENTURY BC)

Love is the joy of the good, the wonder of the wise, the amazement of the Gods.

-PLATO (424/423 BC – 348/347 BC)

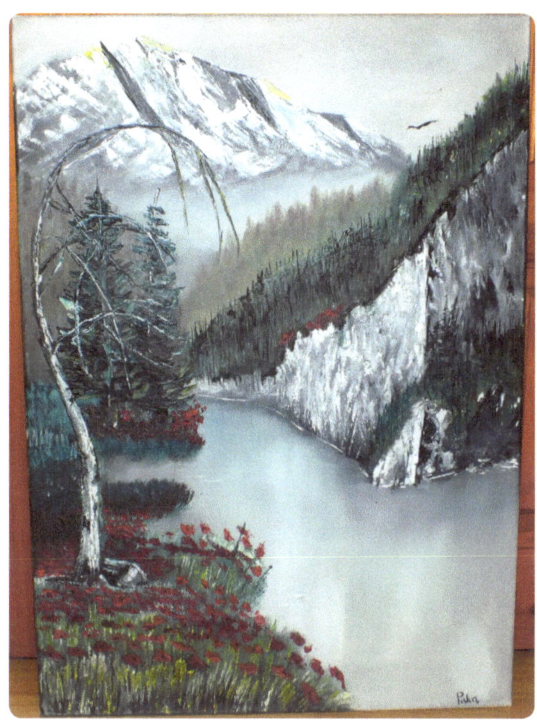

Beata Piska

A loving heart is the beginning of all knowledge.

- THOMAS CARLYLE (1795-1881)

Let us always greet each other with a smile,
for the smile is the beginning of love.

- MOTHER TERESA (1910-1997)

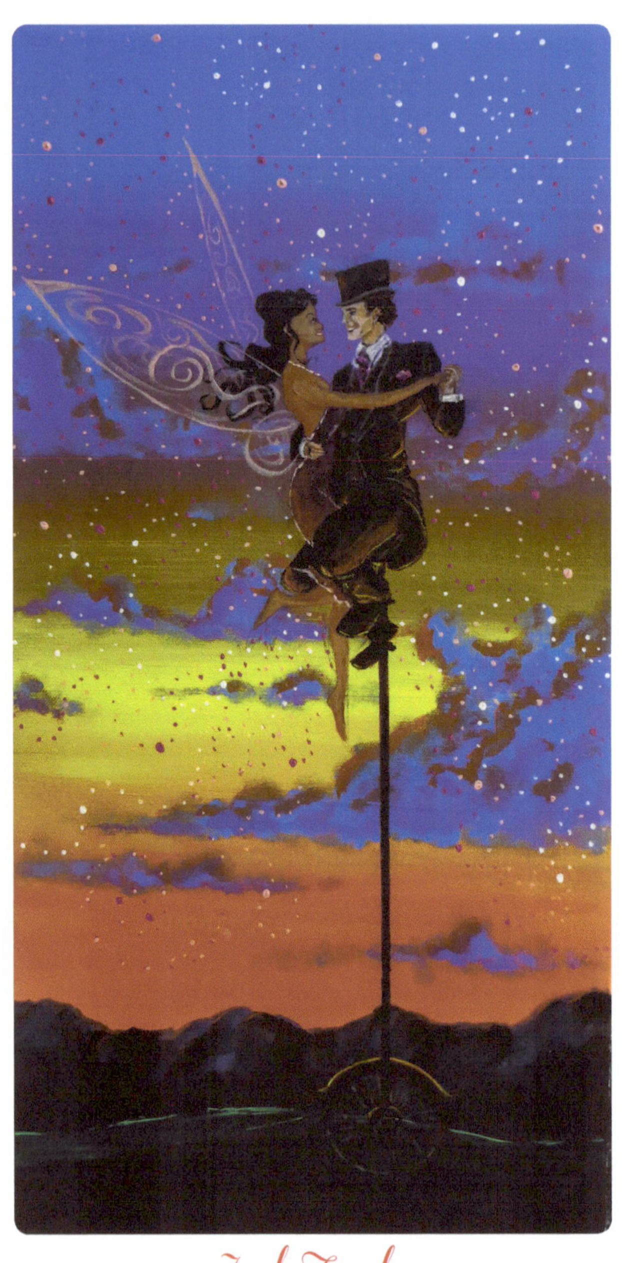

Joel Tesch

Chapter 2
DATING

Computer dating is fine,
if you're a computer

- RITA MAE BROWN (1944 –)

Better that a girl has beauty than brains,
because boys see better than they think.

- JOSH BILLINGS (1818 – 1885)

The world's biggest power is
the youth and beauty of a woman.

- CHANKYA (370 – 283 BC)

Bisexuality immediately doubles your chances
for a date on Saturday night.

- WOODY ALLEN (1935 –)

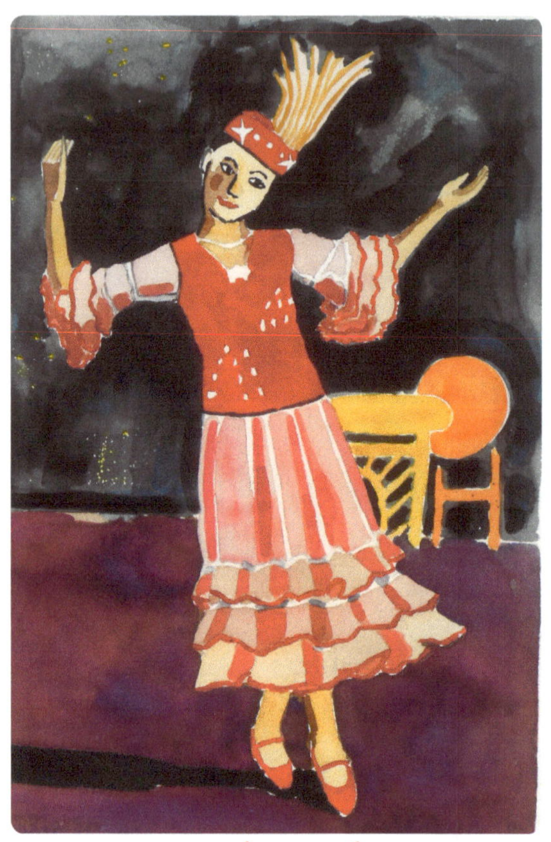

Lesley Giles

In order to avoid being called a flirt, she always yielded easily.

- CHARLES MAURICE DE TALLEYRAND (1754 – 1838)

Chapter 2

DATING

Beauty is in the heart of the beholder.

- H.G. WELLS (1866 – 1946)

Rare is the union of beauty and purity.

- JUVENAL (LATE 1ST AND EARLY 2ND CENTURY AD)

Beauty, more than bitterness,
makes the heart break.

- SARA TEASDALE (1884 – 1933)

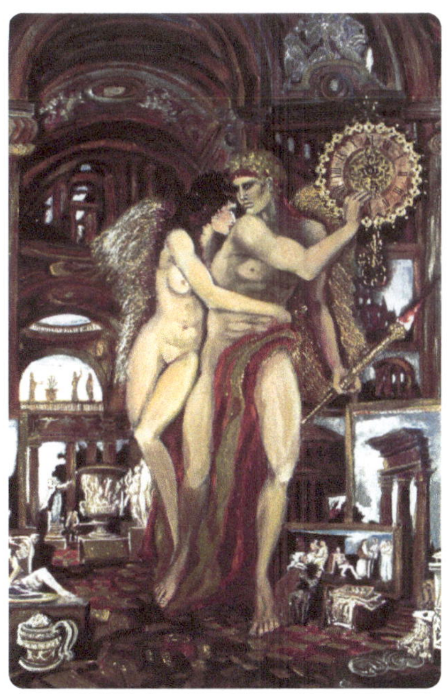

Ione Citrin

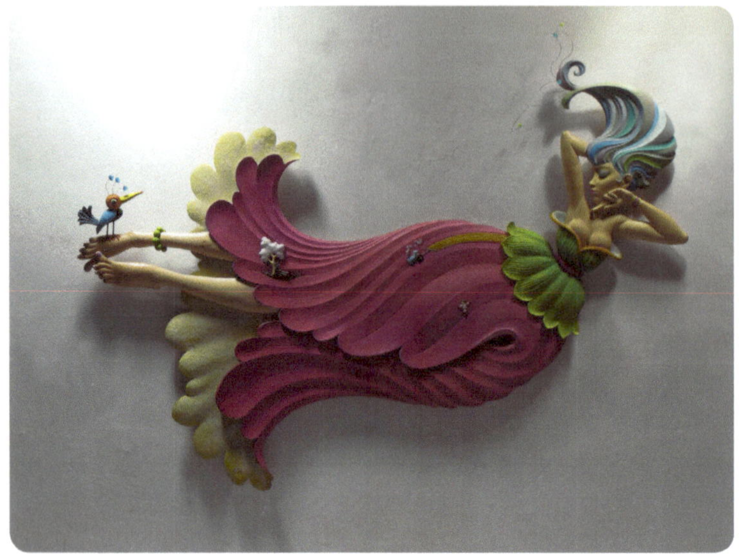

Ferenc Somogyi

Gentlemen prefer blondes,
but take what they can get.

- DON HEROLD (1889 – 1966)

There is a lot to say in her favor,
but the other is more interesting.

- MARK TWAIN (1835 – 1910)

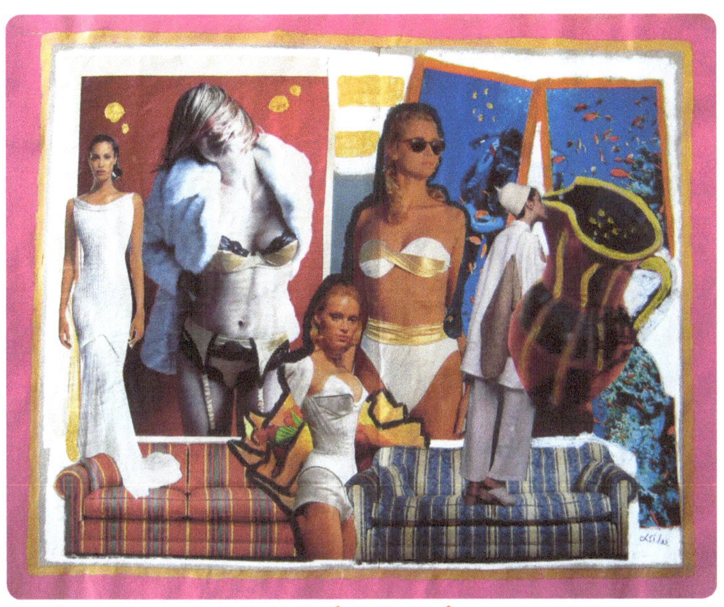

Lesley Giles

Rich widows are the only secondhand goods that sell at first-class prices.

- BENJAMIN FRANKLIN (1706 – 1790)

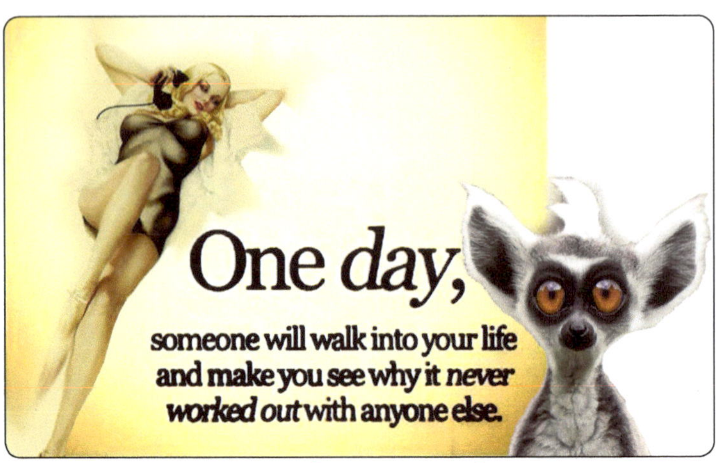

Aida Novosel

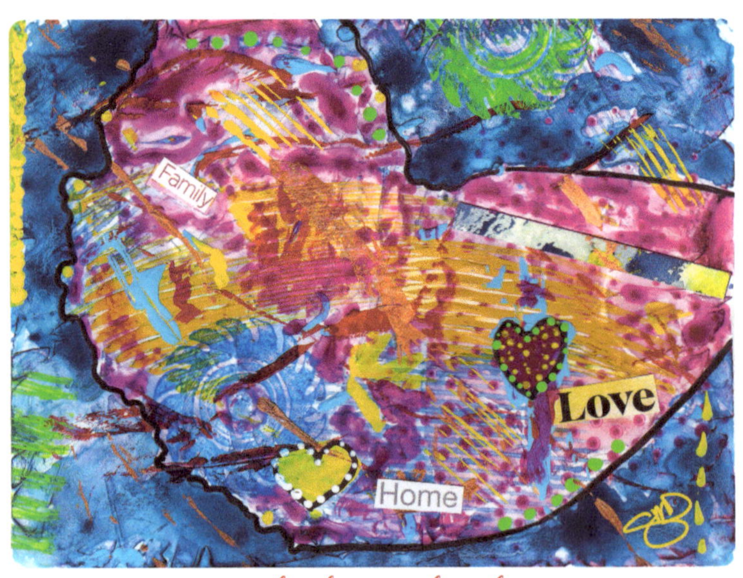

Sheila Delgado

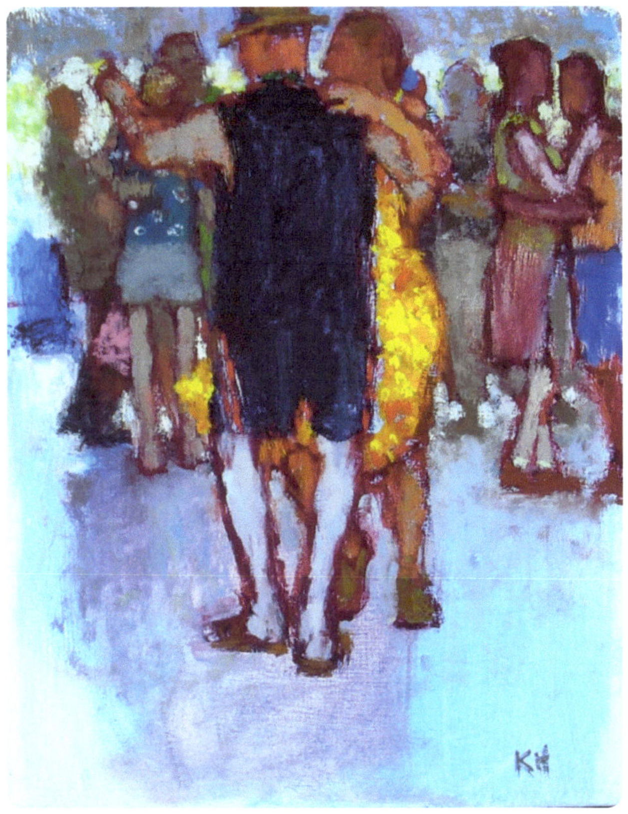

Kate Huntington

Dancing is a perpendicular expression of a horizontal desire.

- GEORGE BERNARD SHAW (1856 – 1950)

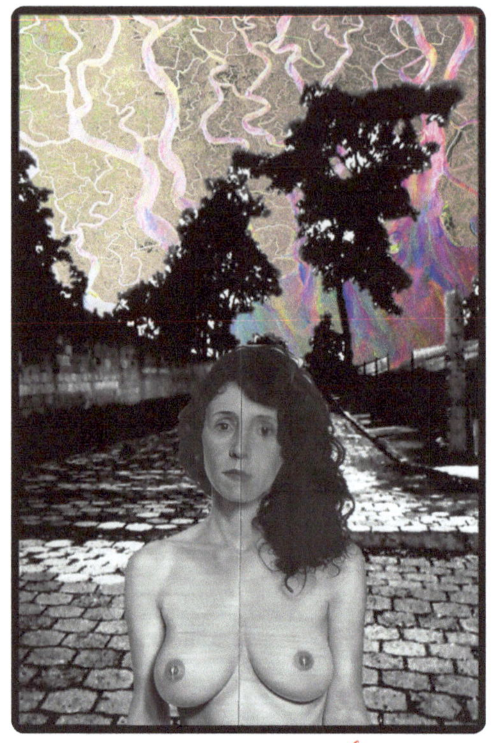

Jimmy Morales

One more drink and I'd be under the host.

- **DOROTHY PARKER** (1893 – 1967)

Drink, pretty creature, drink!

- **WILLIAM WORDSWORTH** (1770 – 1850)

Oh, what lies there are in kisses!

- HEINRICH HEINE (1797 – 1856)

Look for a sweet person. Forget rich.

- ESTEE LAUDER (1908 – 2004)

Beauty is only skin deep.

- THOMAS OVERBURY (1581 – 1613)

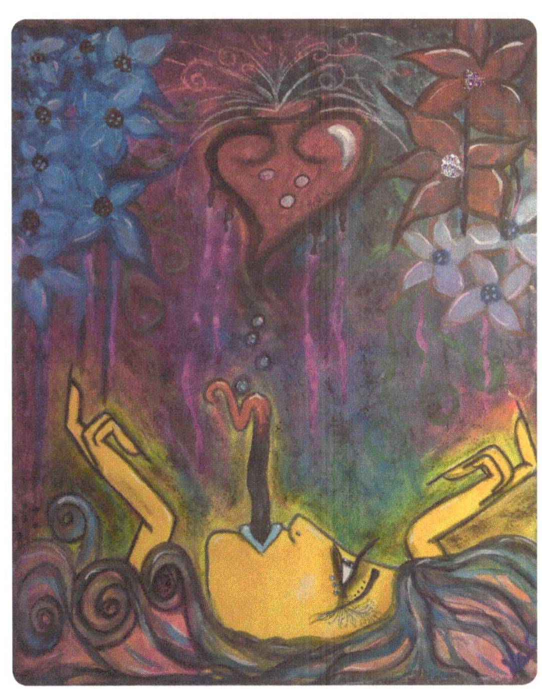

Leslie Rodriguez

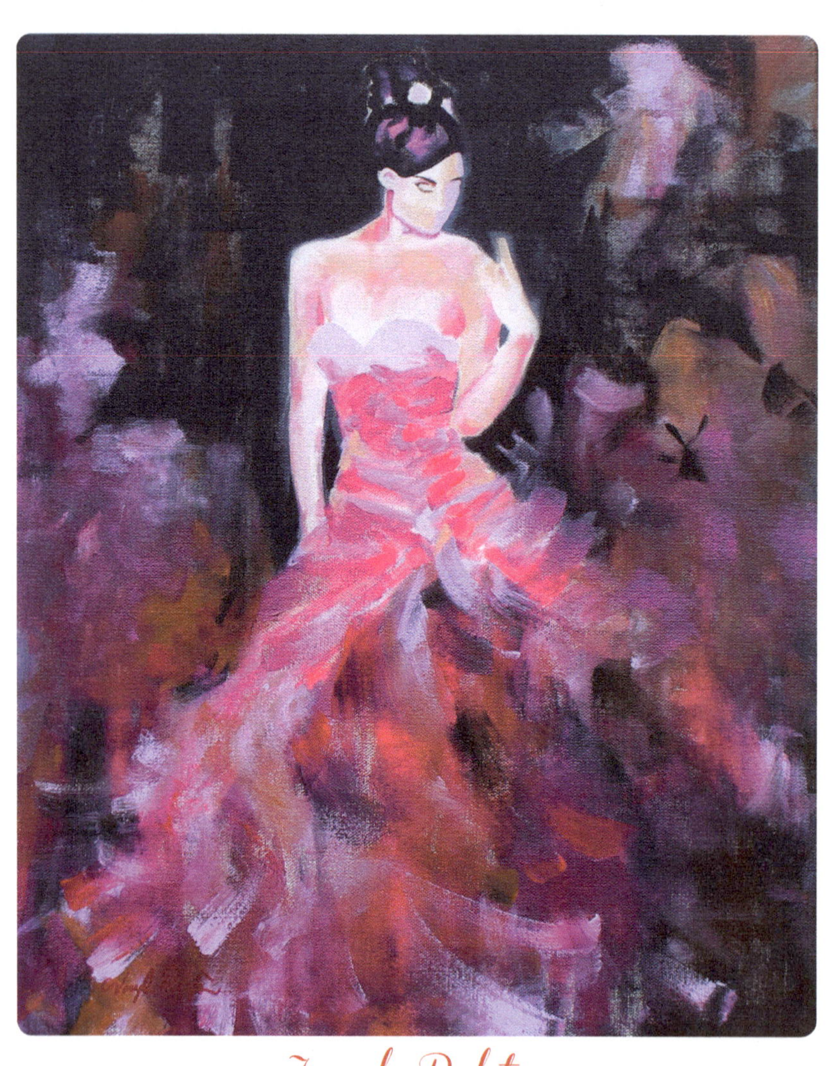

Joseph Palotas

Chapter 3
WOMEN

If women didn't exist, all the money in the world would have no meaning.

- ARISTOTLE ONASSIS (1906 – 1975)

Brains are an asset, if you hide them.

- MAE WEST (1892 – 1980)

Good girls go to heaven, bad girls go everywhere.

- HELEN GURLEY BROWN (1922 – 2012)

Women are meant to be loved, not to be understood.

- OSCAR WILDE (1854 – 1900)

**She got her good looks from her father.
He's a plastic surgeon.**

- GROUCHO MARX (1890 – 1977)

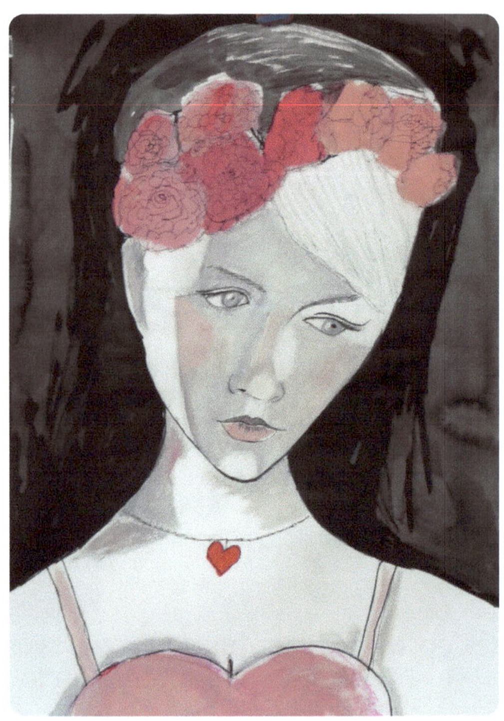

Carolyn Schlam

She's the kind of girl who climbed the ladder of success wrong by wrong.

- MAE WEST (1892 – 1980)

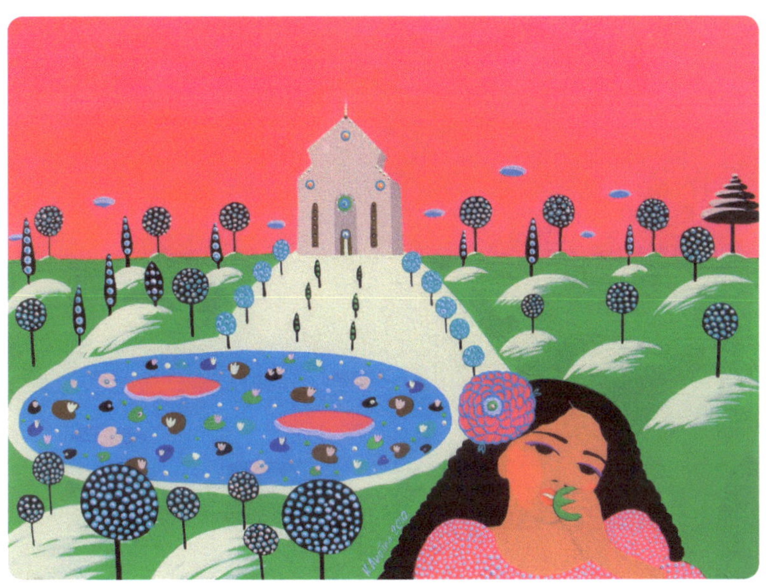

Katrina Avotina

Who loves not women, wine, and song remains a fool his whole life long.

- MARTIN LUTHER (1483 – 1546)

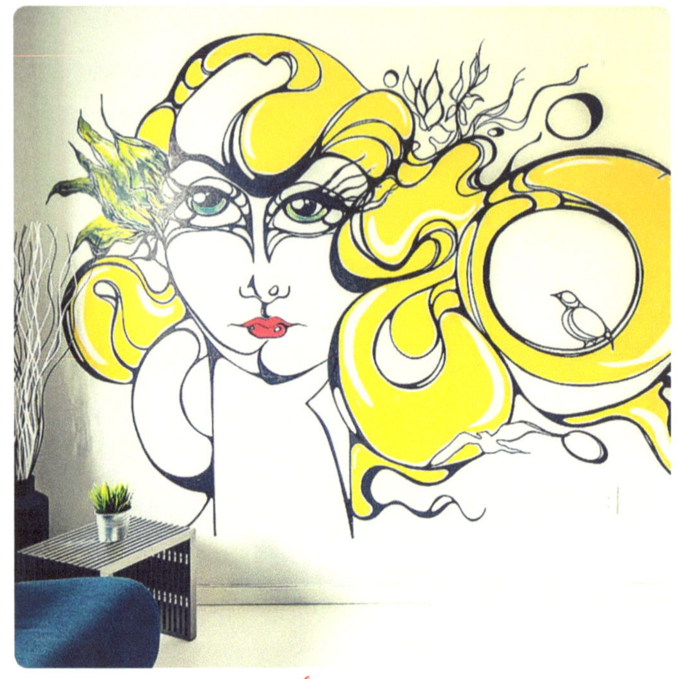

Marlene Jorge

There is a lot to say in her favor,
but the other is more interesting.

- MARK TWAIN (1835 – 1910)

No cavalry or infantry has gall
to maneuver as coolly as a woman can.

- TITUS MACCIUS PLAUTUS (255 – 184 BC)

Chapter 3
WOMEN

Women are like elephants to me,
I like to look at 'em but I wouldn't want to own one.

- W. C. FIELDS (1880 – 1946)

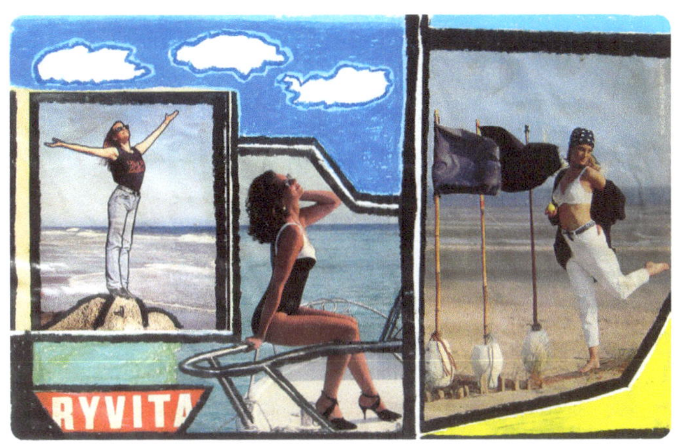

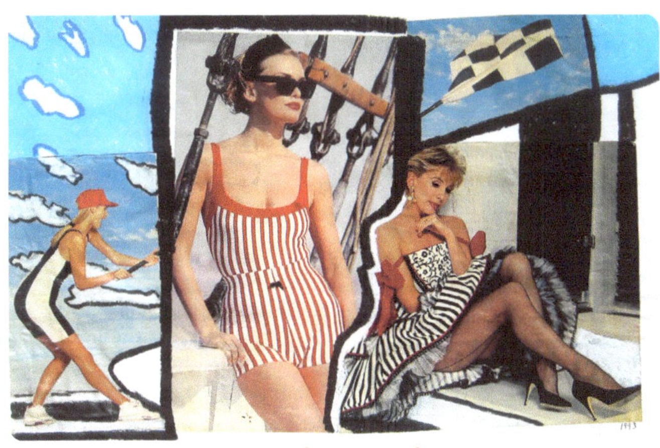

Lesley Giles

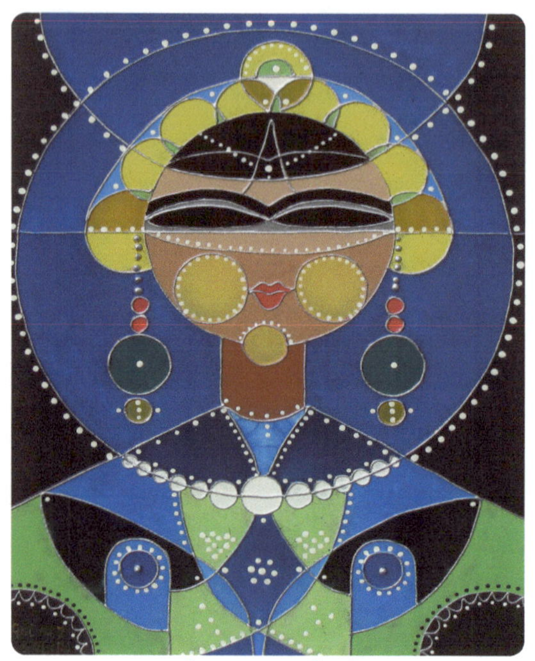

Golnaz Shobeiri

I don't know anything better than a woman,
if you want to spend money where it'll show.

- FRANK MCKINNEY "KIN" HUBBARD (1868 – 1930)

Woman is surely the daughter of delay.

- TITUS MACCIUS PLAUTUS (255 – 184 BC)

Chapter 3
WOMEN

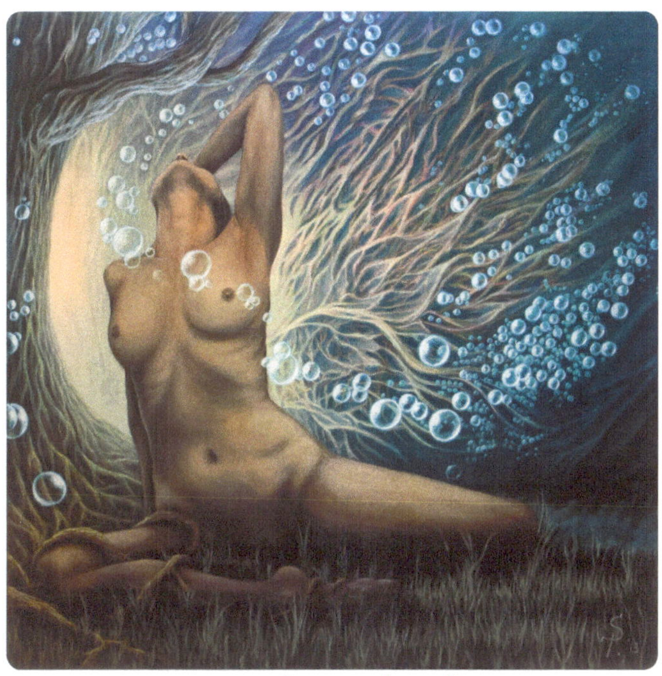

Paul Sadowski

Of all the wild beasts of land or sea,
the wildest is women.

- MENANDER (342 – 291 BC)

Women want mediocre men, and men are working hard to become as mediocre as possible.

– MARGARET MEAD (1901 – 1978)

If women are expected to do the same work as men, we must teach them the same things.

- PLATO (424/423BC – 348/347BC)

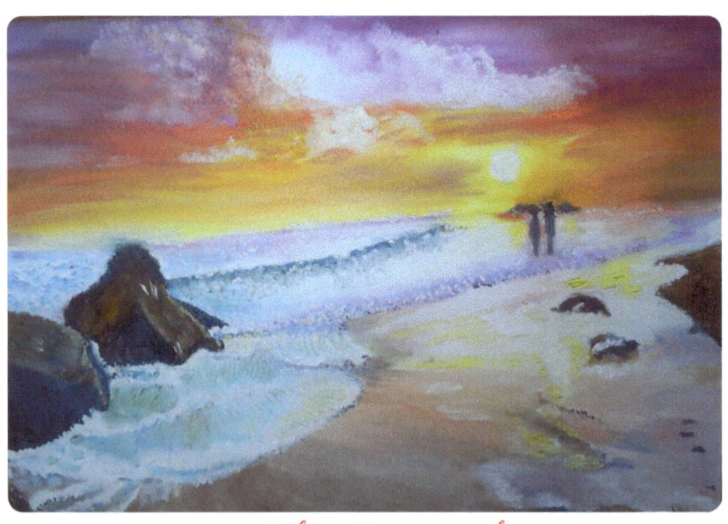

Adri Barnard

The thing women have yet to learn is nobody gives you power. You just take it.

- ROSEANNE BARR (1952 –)

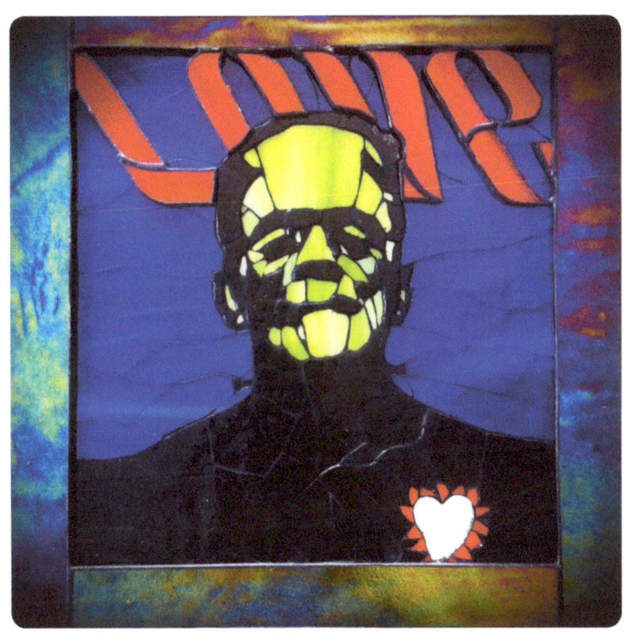

Yalily Mejïa

At the age of eleven or thereabout women acquire a poise and ability to handle difficult situations which a man, if he is lucky manages to achieve somewhere in the later seventies.

– P. G. WODEHOUSE (1881 – 1975)

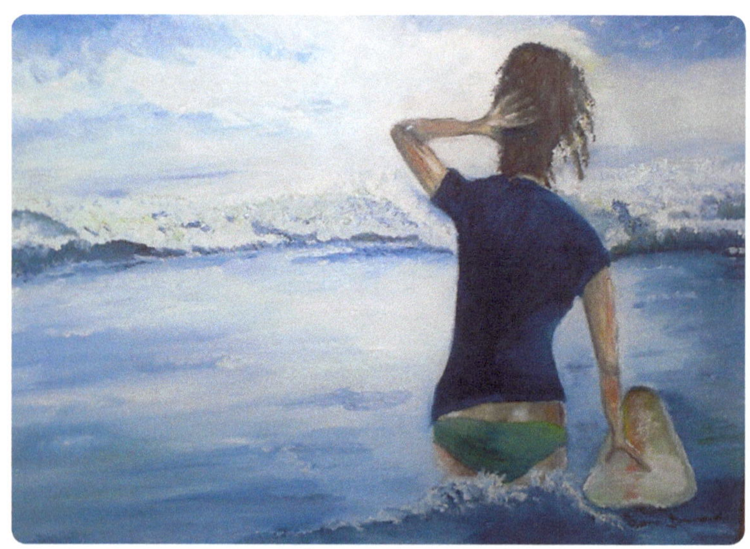

Adri Barnard

Chapter 3
WOMEN

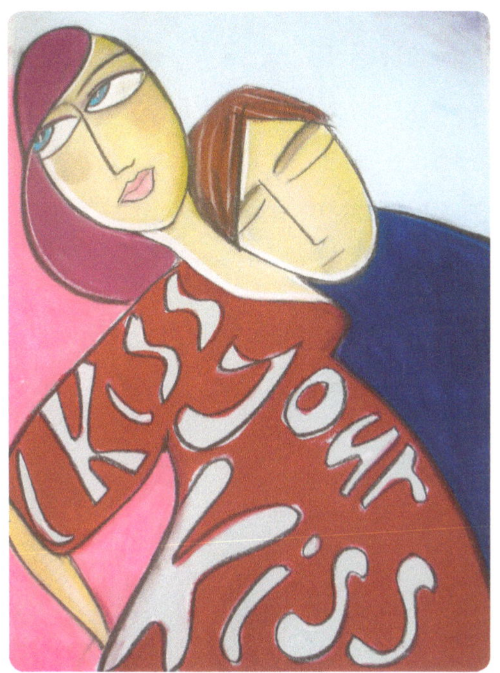

Samantha Thompson

Whether they give or refuse,
it delights women just the same to be asked.

– OVID (43 BC – 17 AD)

Women with pasts interest men…
they hope history will repeat itself.

– MAE WEST (1892 – 1980)

How hard it is for women to keep counsel!

– WILLIAM SHAKESPEARE (1564 – 1616)

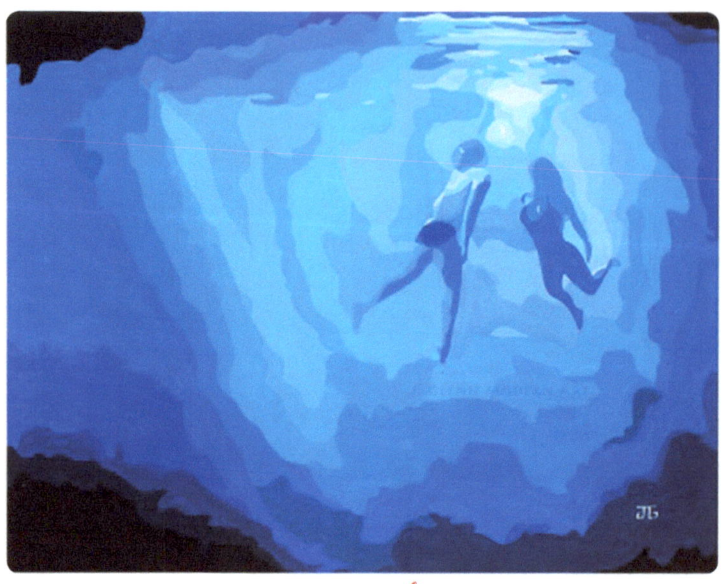

Jesse Glenn

Women prefer men who have something tender about them—especially the legal kind.

– KAY INGRAM (19?? –)

Chapter 3
WOMEN

**God gave women intuition and femininity.
Used properly, the combination easily jumbles
the brain of any man I've ever met.**

– FARRAH FAWCETT (1947 – 2009)

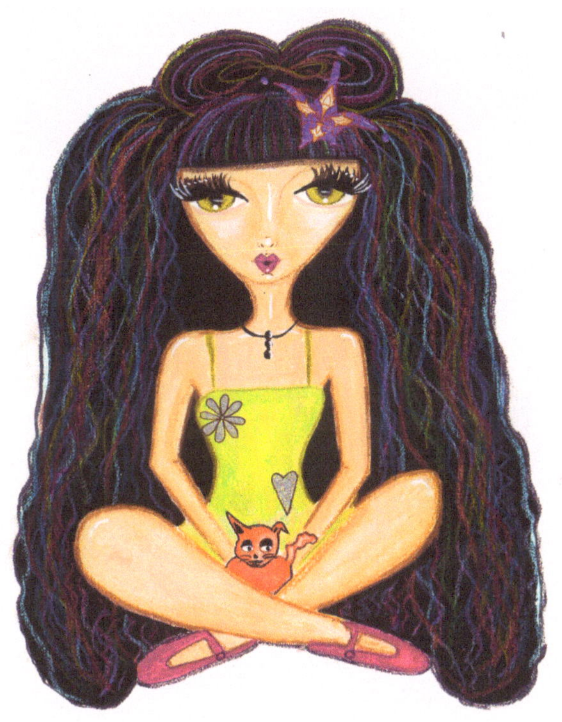

Leslie Rodriguez

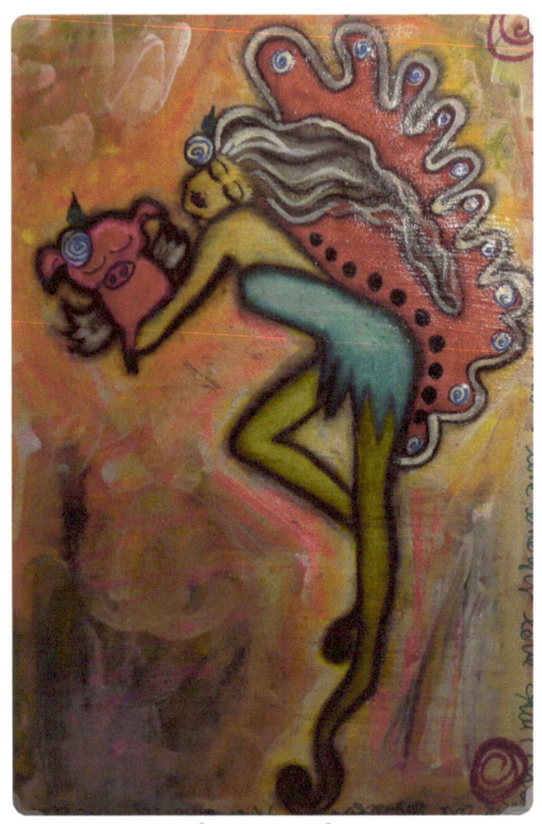

Leslie Rodriguez

I love the women's movement... especially when I'm walking behind it.

- RUSH LIMBAUGH (1951 –)

But never fear, gentlemen;
castration was never really not the point
of feminism, and we women are too busy
eviscerating one another to take you on.

- ANNA QUINDLEN (1953 –)

Women and cats do as they damned well please,
and men and dogs had best learn to live with it.

- ALAN HOLBROOK

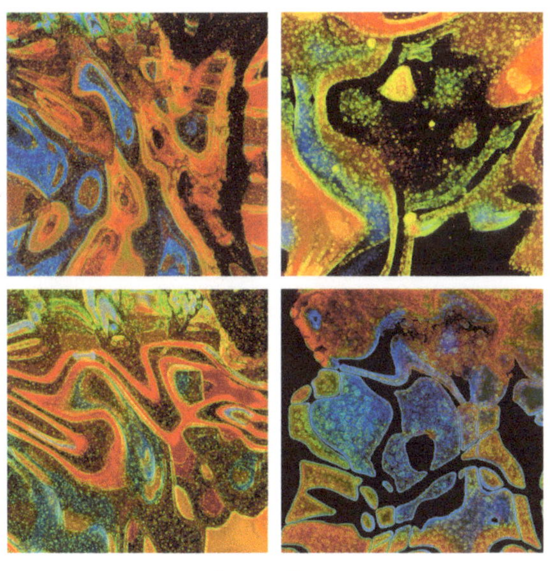

Carlos de Jong

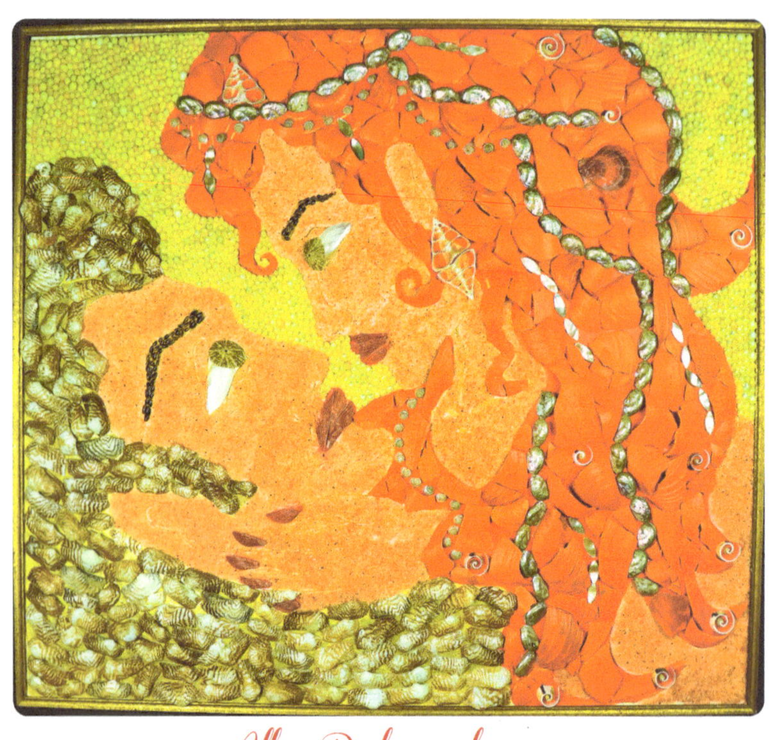

Alla Baksanskaya

Chapter 4
MEN

It's not the men in your life that matters,
it's the life in your men.

- MAE WEST (1892 – 1980)

A boy is, of all wild beasts,
the most difficult to manage.

- PLATO (424/423 – 348/347 BC)

In politics, if you want anything said, ask a man.
If you want anything done, ask a woman.

- MARGARET THATCHER (1925 – 2013)

Men should think twice before making
widowhood women's only path to power.

- GLORIA STEINEM (1934 –)

See, the problem is that God gives men a brain and a penis, and only enough blood to run one at a time.

- ROBIN WILLIAMS (1951 – 2014)

Sometimes I wonder if men and women really suit each other. Perhaps they should live next door and just visit now and then.

- KATHARINE HEPBURN (1907 – 2003)

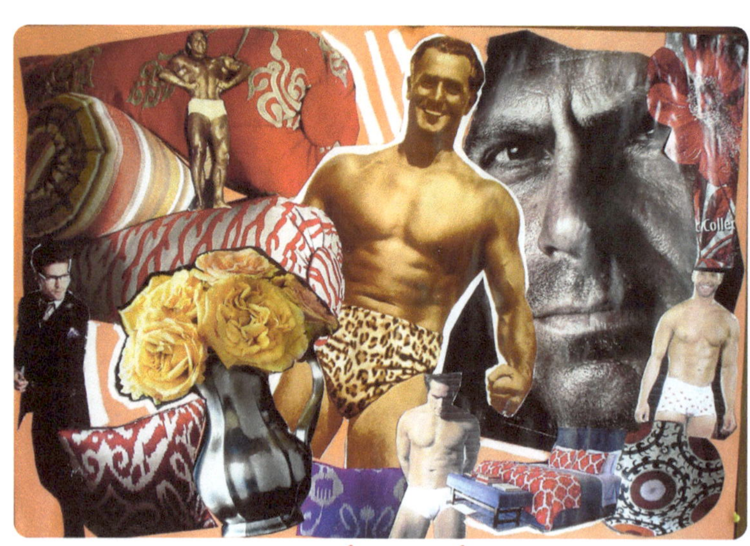

Lesley Giles

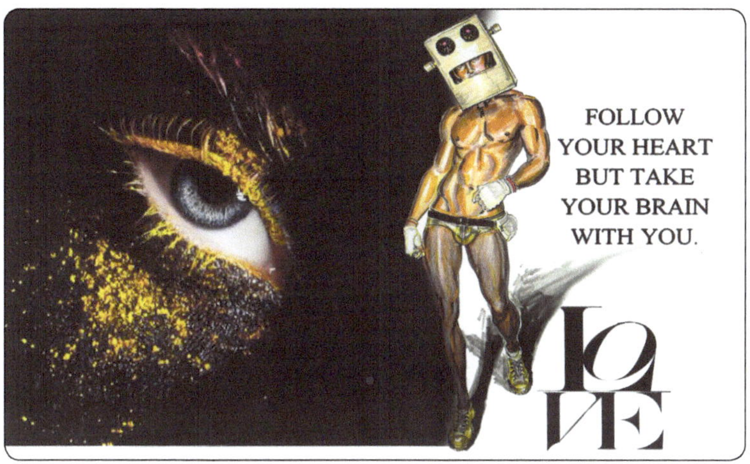

Aida Novosel

A woman's guess is much more accurate than a man's certainty.

- RUDYARD KIPLING (1865 – 1936)

We have reason to believe that man first walked upright to free his hands for masturbation.

- LILY TOMLIN (1939 –)

Men are as faithful as their options.

- CHRIS ROCK (1965 –)

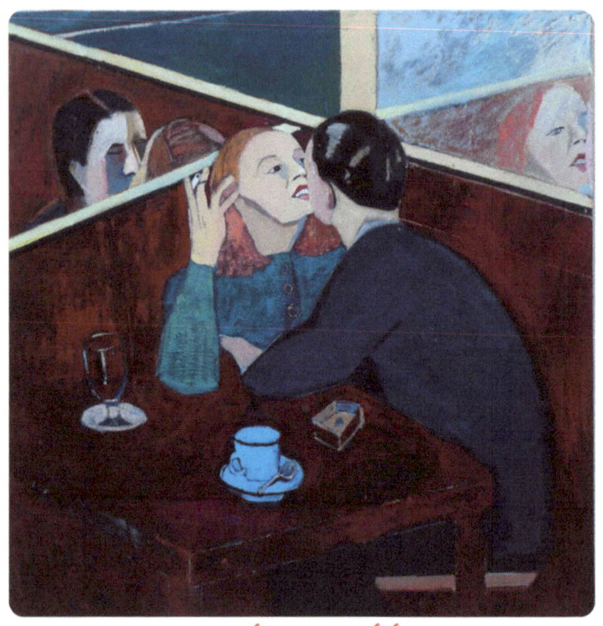

Carolyn Schlam

I never hated a man enough
to give him his diamonds back.

- ZSA ZSA GABOR (1917 –)

Here's all you have to know about men and women:
women are crazy, men are stupid. And the main
reason women are crazy is that men are stupid.

- GEORGE CARLIN (1937 – 2008)

As usual, there is a great woman behind every idiot.

- JOHN LENNON (1940 – 1980)

Every man I meet wants to protect me.
I can't figure out what from.

- MAE WEST (1892 – 1980)

Men didn't respect beauty...they used it.

- NORA ROBERTS (1950 –)

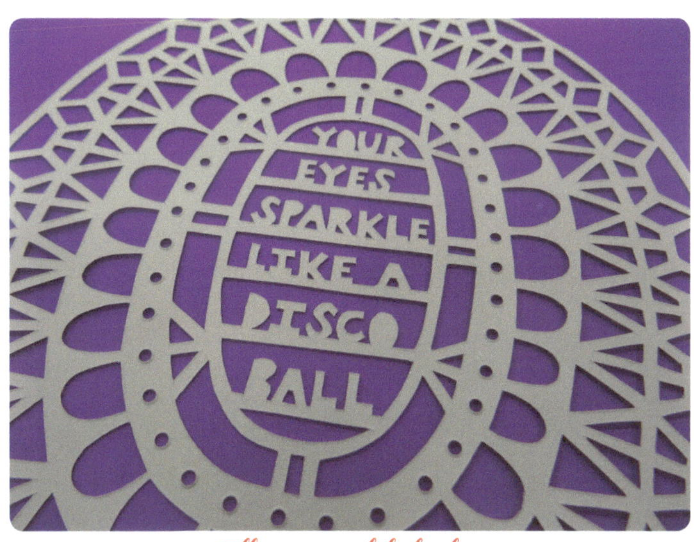

Ellen Schlobohm

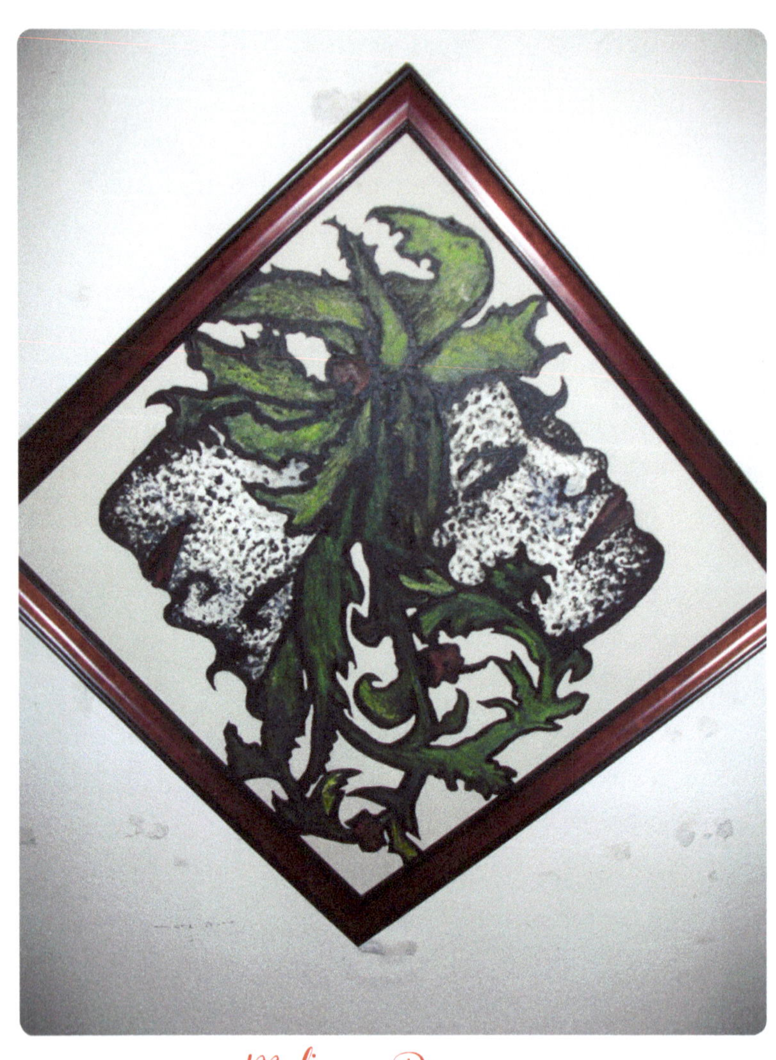

Melissa Bruneau

Chapter 5

SEX

I can remember when the air was clean
and sex was dirty.

- GEORGE BURNS (1896 – 1996)

A man can no more separate age and covetousness
than he can part young limbs and lechery...

- WILLIAM SHAKESPEARE (1564 – 1616)

Sex is good,
but not as good as fresh sweet corn.

- GARRISON KEILLOR (1942 –)

My brain is my second favorite organ.

- WOODY ALLEN (1935 –)

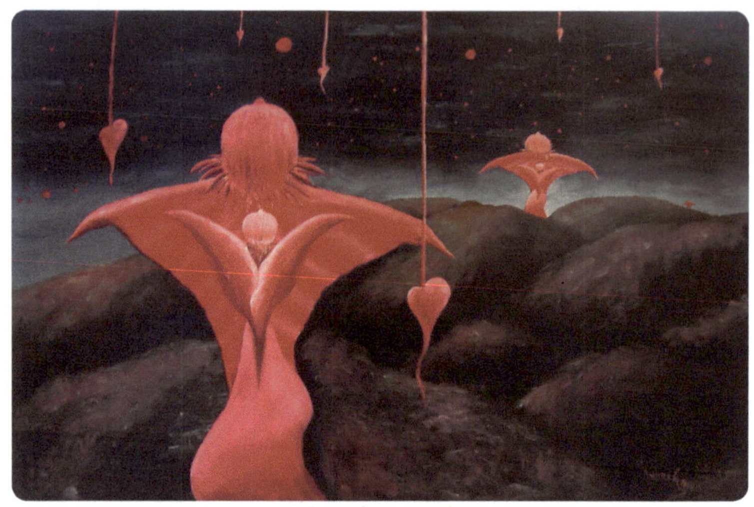

Lubosh Valenta

It is one of the superstitions of the human mind to have imagined that virginity could be a virtue.

- VOLTAIRE (1694 – 1778)

Of all the sexual aberrations
the most peculiar is chastity.

- REMY DE GOURMONT (1858 – 1915)

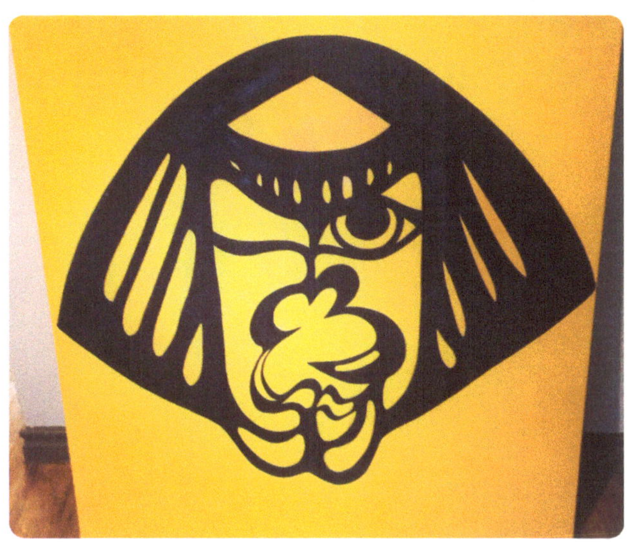

Marlene Jorge

If men could get pregnant,
abortion would be a sacrament.

- FLORYNCE "FLO" KENNEDY (1916 – 2000)

Dear Lord, give me chastity and self-restraint, but not yet.

- SAINT AUGUSTINE (354 – 430)

Sex alleviates tension. Love causes it.

- WOODY ALLEN (1935 –)

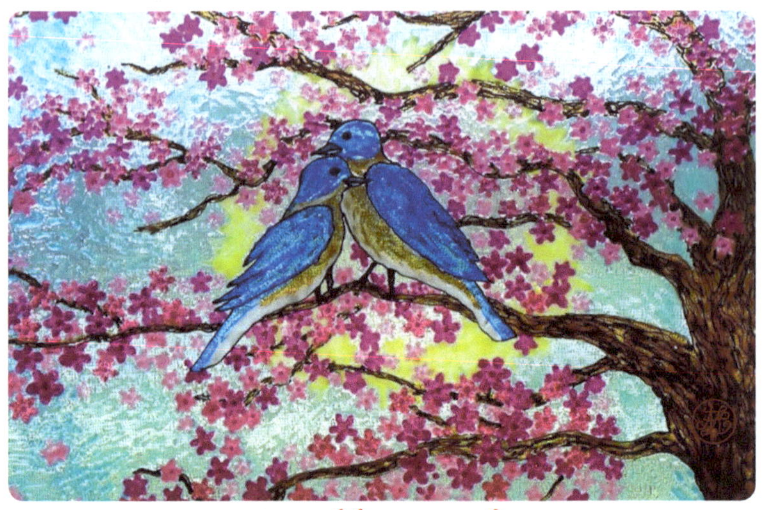

Angelika Parker

If it is worth doing,
it is worth doing slowly … very slowly.

- GYPSY ROSE LEE (1911/1914 – 1970)

You gotta learn that if you don't get it by midnight, chances are you ain't gonna get it; and if you do, it ain't worth it.

- CASEY STENGEL (1890 – 1975)

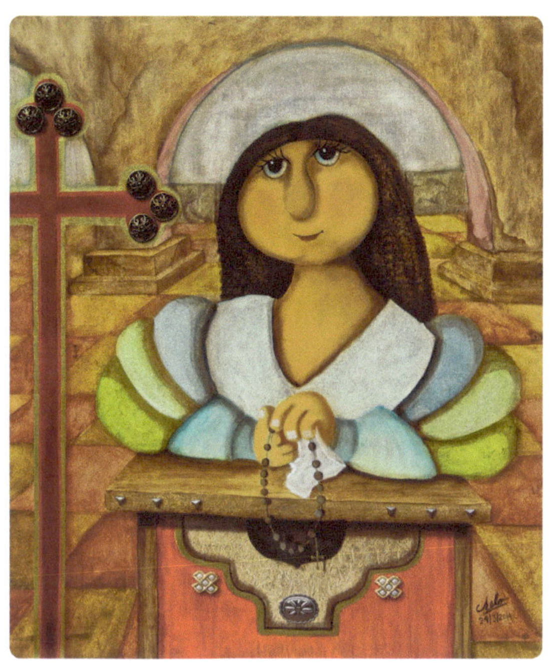

Chelo Gonzalez

Why should we take advice on sex from the pope?
If he knows anything about it, he shouldn't.

- GEORGE BERNARD SHAW (1856 – 1950)

The big difference between sex for money and sex for free is that sex for money usually costs a lot less.

- BRENDAN BEHAN (1923 – 1964)

**Whoever called it necking
was a poor judge of anatomy.**

- GROUCHO MARX (1890 – 1977)

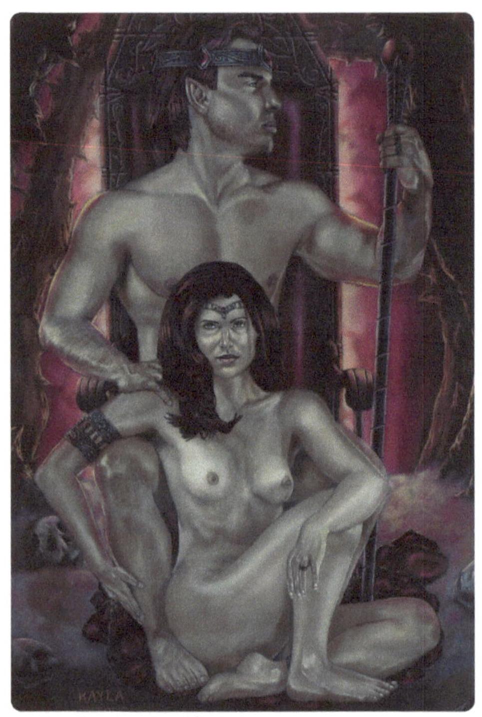

Kayla Ascencio

Masturbation! The amazing availability of it.

- JAMES JOYCE (1882 – 1941)

The good thing about masturbation is you don't have to dress up for it.

- TRUMAN CAPOTE (1924 – 1984)

Hey! Don't knock masturbation. It's sex with someone I love.

- WOODY ALLEN (1935 –)

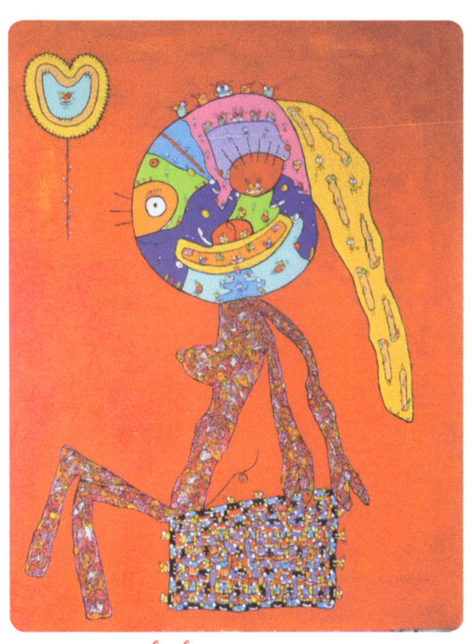

Vhilo Persson

If only it was as easy to banish hunger by rubbing the belly as it is to masturbate.

- DIOGENES "THE CYNIC" (412 – 323 BC)

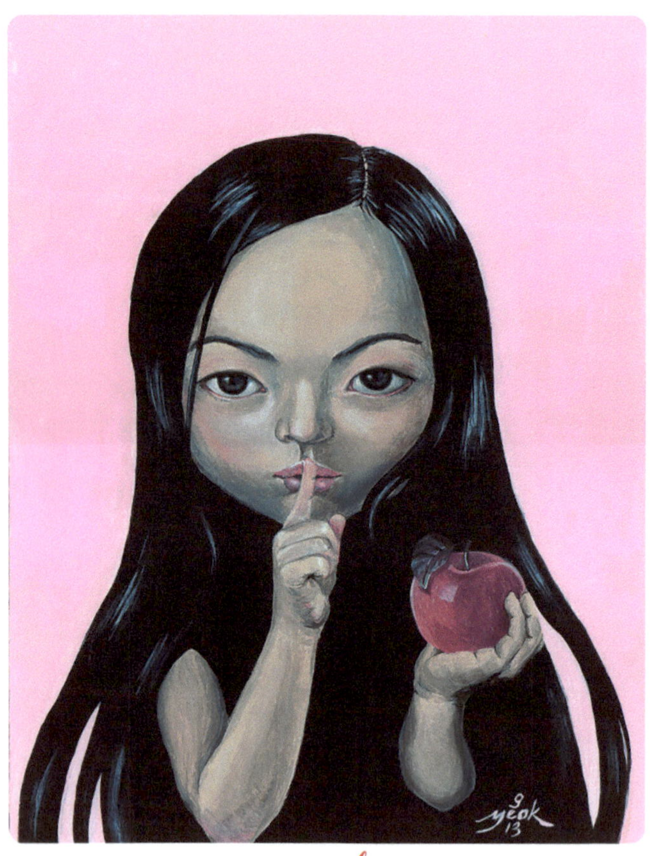

Yeok

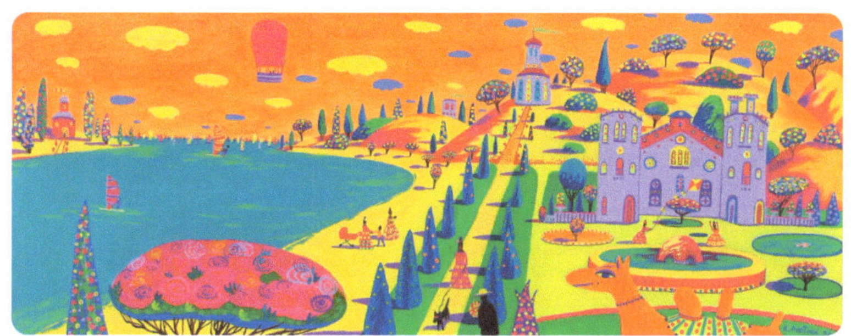

Katrina Avotina

Is it not strange that desire should
so many years outlive performance?

- WILLIAM SHAKESPEARE (1564 – 1616)

Immorality: the morality of those
who are having a better time.

- H. L. MENCKEN (1880 – 1956)

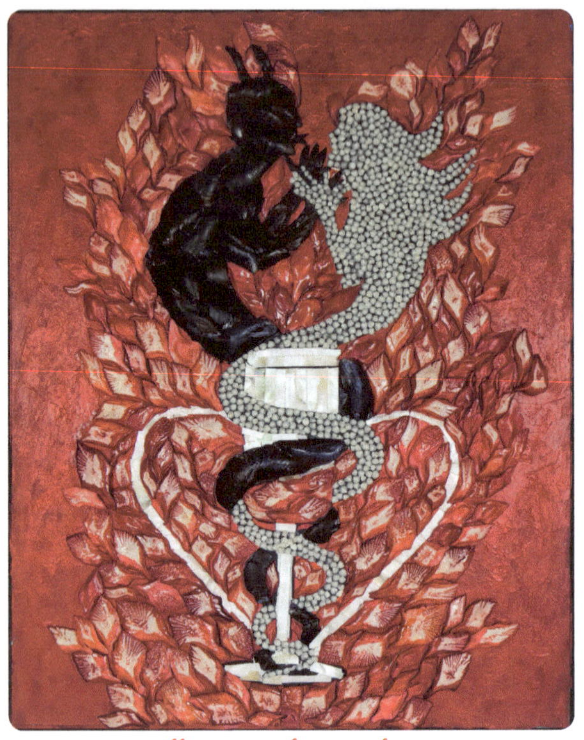

Alla Baksanskaya

Sex: The thing that takes up the least amount of time and causes the most amount of trouble.

- JOHN BARRYMORE (1882 – 1942)

Familiarity breeds contempt – and children.

- MARK TWAIN (1835 – 1910)

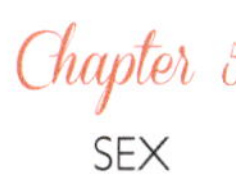

Chapter 5
SEX

The pleasure is momentary, the position ridiculous, and the expense damnable.

- LORD CHESTERFIELD (1694 – 1773)

Power is the ultimate aphrodisiac.

- HENRY KISSINGER (1923 –)

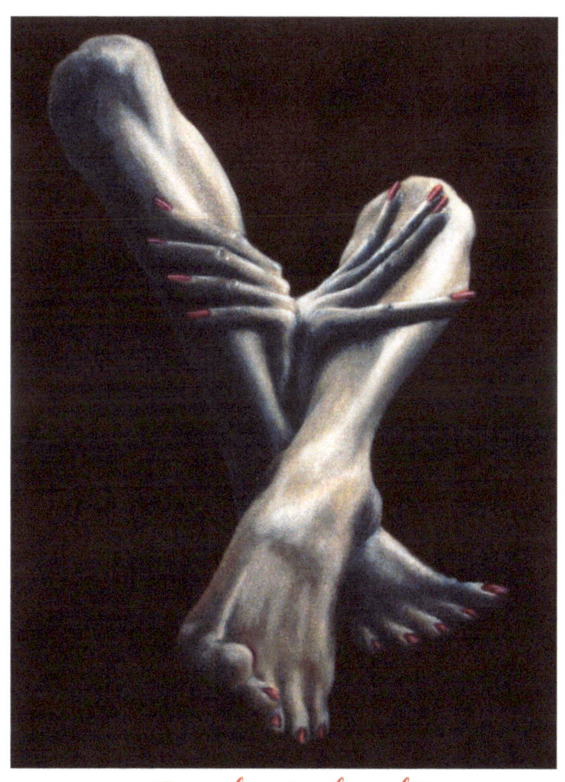

Paul Sadowski

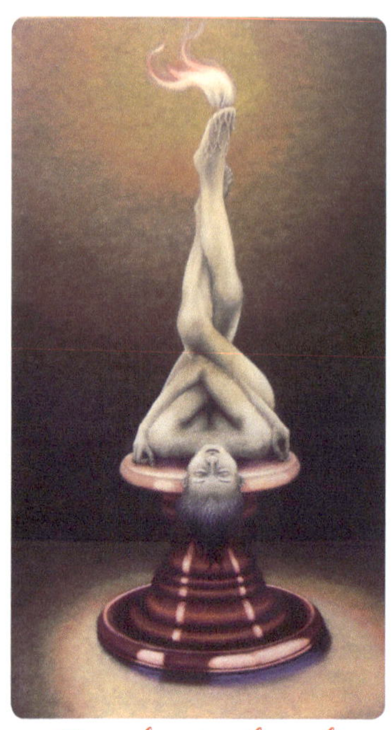

Paul Sadowski

Remember if you smoke after sex, you're doing it too fast.

- WOODY ALLEN (1935 –)

Lust wants what it can't have.

- PUBLILIUS SYRUS (85 – 43 BC)

Sex without love is an empty experience,
but, as empty experiences go it's one of the best.

- WOODY ALLEN (1935 –)

When choosing between two evils,
I always like to take the one I've never tried before.

- MAE WEST (1892 – 1980)

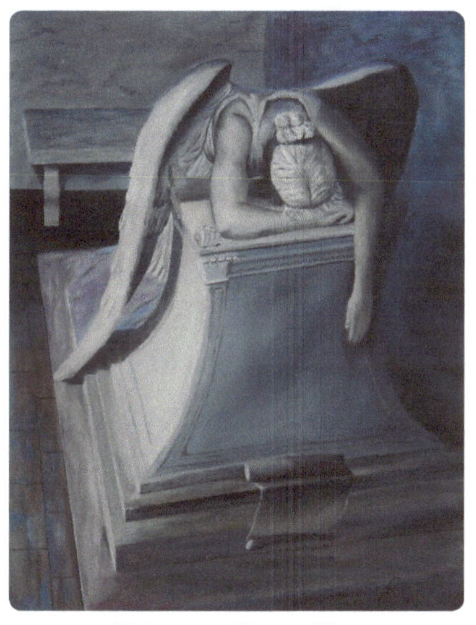

Gino Di Dio

Tell him I've been too fucking busy – or vice versa.

- DOROTHY PARKER (1893 – 1967)

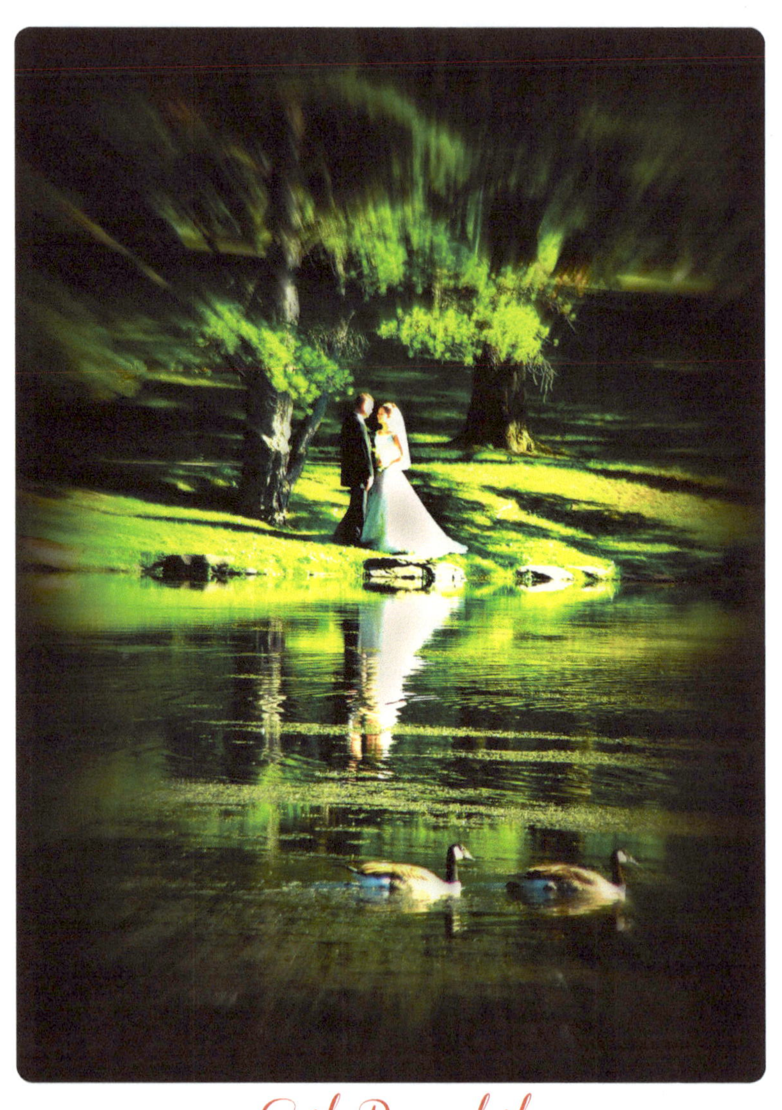

Earl Devendorf

The husband who wants a happy marriage should learn to keep his mouth shut and his checkbook open.

- GROUCHO MARX (1890 – 1977)

Husbands are like fires. They go out if unattended.

- ZSA ZSA GABOR (1917 –)

Husbands never become good;
they merely become proficient.

- H. L. MENCKEN (1880 – 1956)

My wife was too beautiful for words
but not for arguments.

- JOHN BARRYMORE (1882 – 1942)

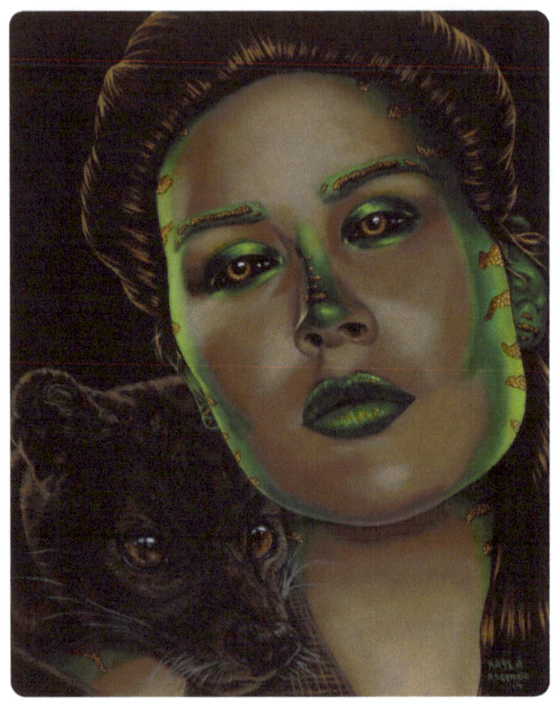

Kayla Ascencio

Woman begins by resisting a man's advances and ends by blocking his retreat.

- OSCAR WILDE (1854 – 1900)

Marriage is really tough because you have to deal with feelings and lawyers.

- RICHARD PRYOR (1940 – 2005)

Chapter 6

MARRIAGE

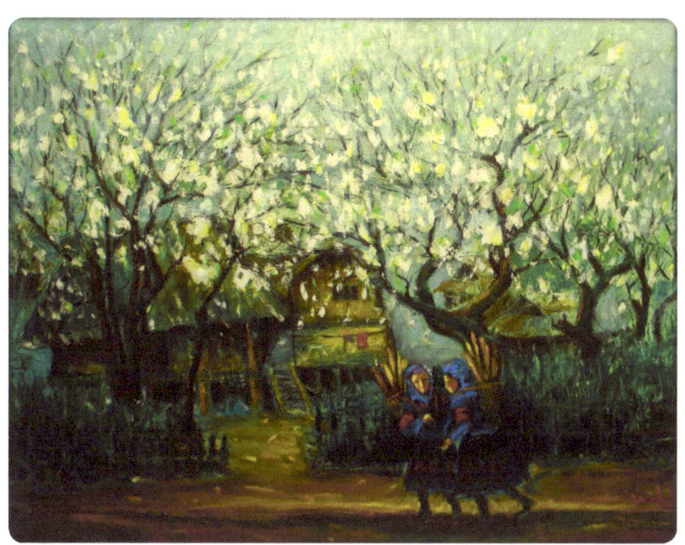

Ninh Le

"Home Sweet Home" must surely
have been written by a bachelor.

- SAMUEL BUTLER (1835 – 1902)

By all means, marry.
If you get a good wife, you'll become happy;
if you get a bad wife, you'll become a philosopher.

- SOCRATES (470 – 399 BC)

A woman usually respects her father, but her view of her husband is mingled with contempt, for she is, of course, privy to the transparent devices by which she snared him.

- H. L. MENCKEN (1880 – 1956)

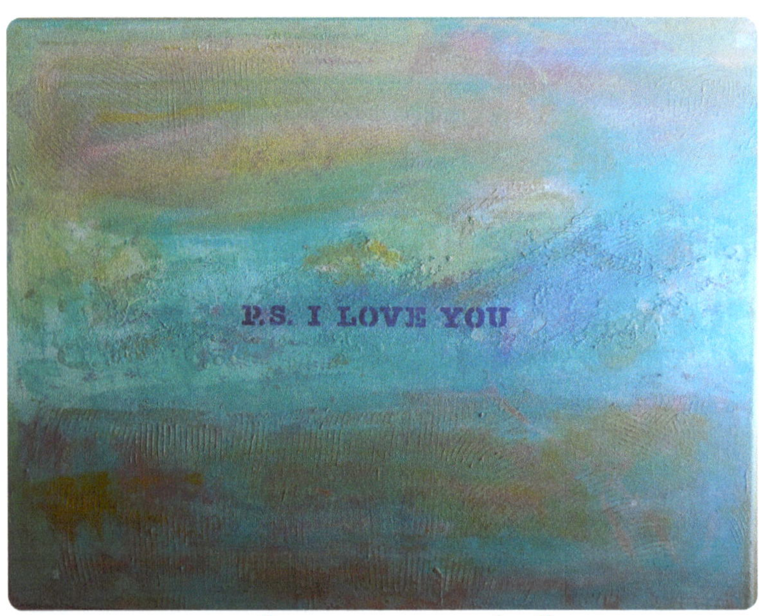

Christine Marshall

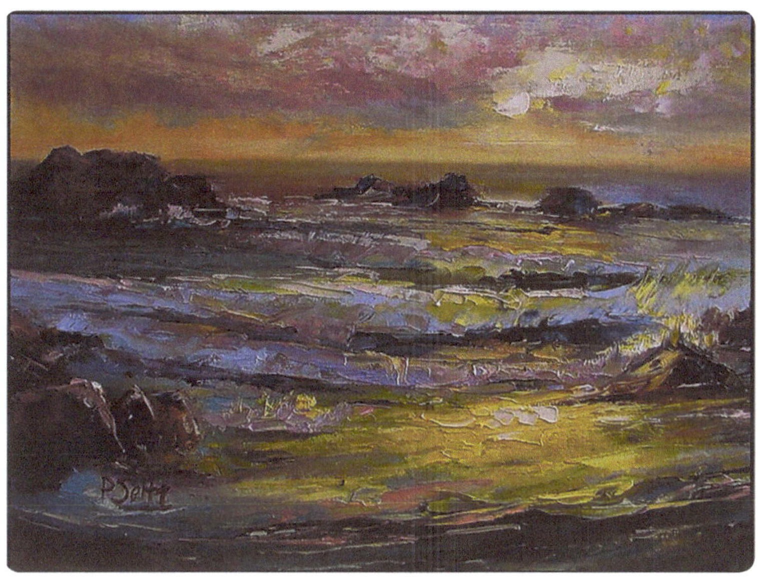

Patricia Elliott Seitz

A dowry is a wonderful source of money,
only if it comes without the wife.

- TITUS MACCIUS PLAUTUS (255 – 184 BC)

American women expect to find in their husbands
a perfection that English women only hope
to find in their butlers.

- W. SOMERSET MAUGHAM (1874 – 1965)

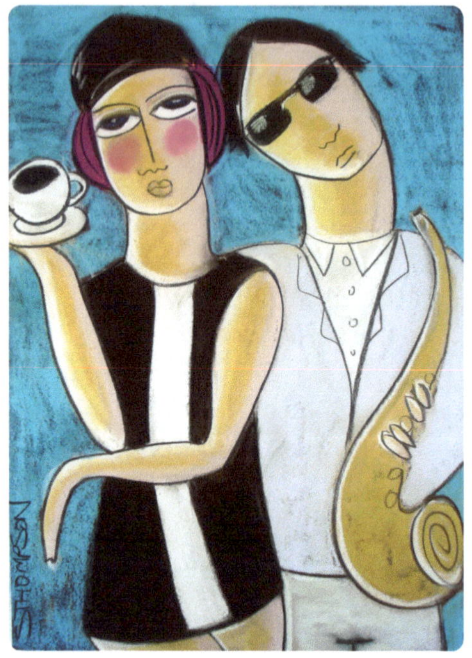

Samantha Thompson

I wonder if the screwing I'm getting
is worth the screwing I'm getting.

- LANA TURNER (1921 – 1995)

Marriage is a great institution but I'm not ready
for an institution yet. Whenever you want to
marry someone, go have lunch with his ex-wife.

- SHELLEY WINTERS (1920 – 2006)

The trouble with some women is that they get all excited about nothing – and then marry him.

- CHER (1946 –)

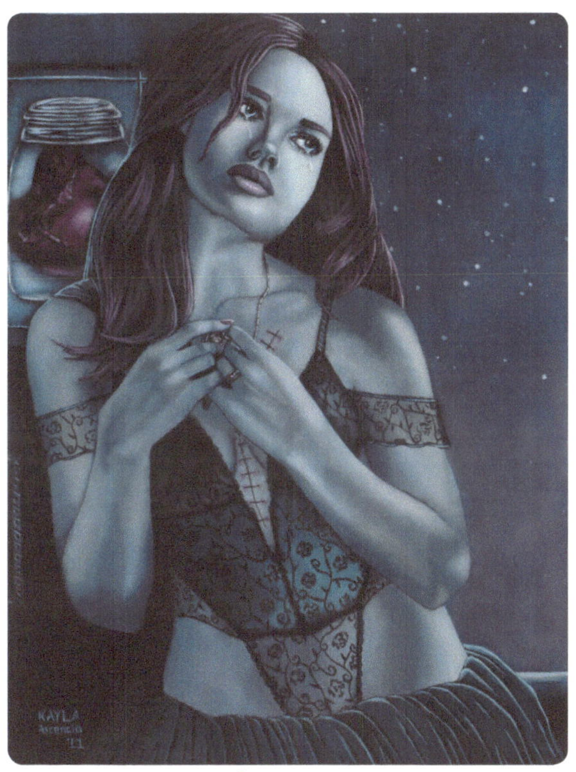

Kayla Ascencio

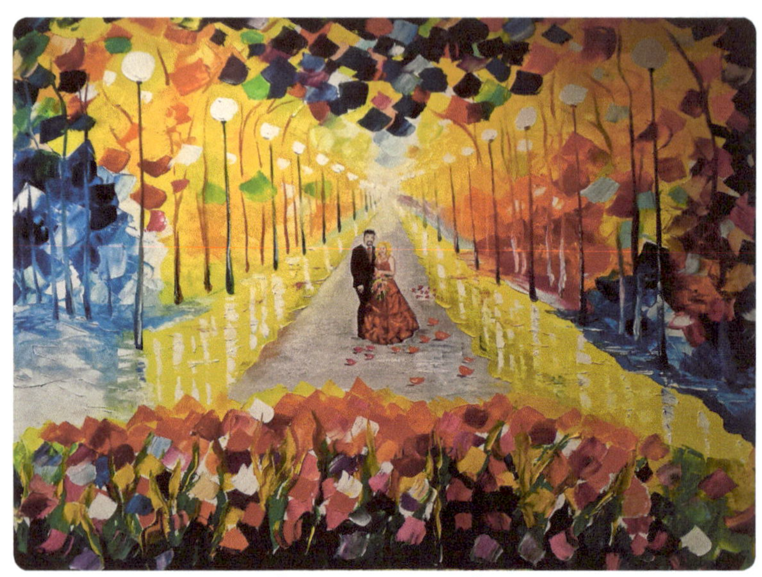

Eleonora Pulcini

I have learned that only two things are necessary to keep one's wife happy. First, let her think she's having her way, and second, let her have it.

- LYNDON B. JOHNSON (1908 – 1973)

Chapter 6
MARRIAGE

**Marriage is popular because it combines
the maximum of temptation
with the maximum of opportunity.**

- GEORGE BERNARD SHAW (1856 – 1950)

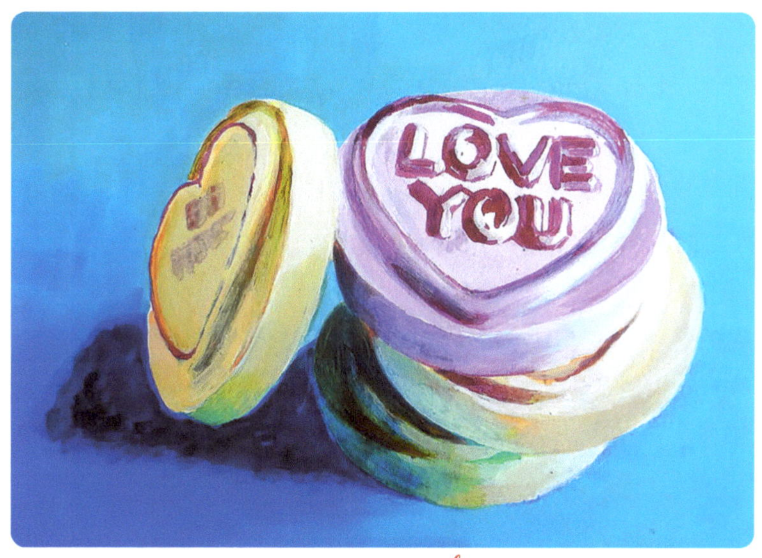

Sue Gardner

It's a funny thing that when a man hasn't anything on earth to worry about, he goes off and gets married.

- ROBERT FROST (1874 – 1963)

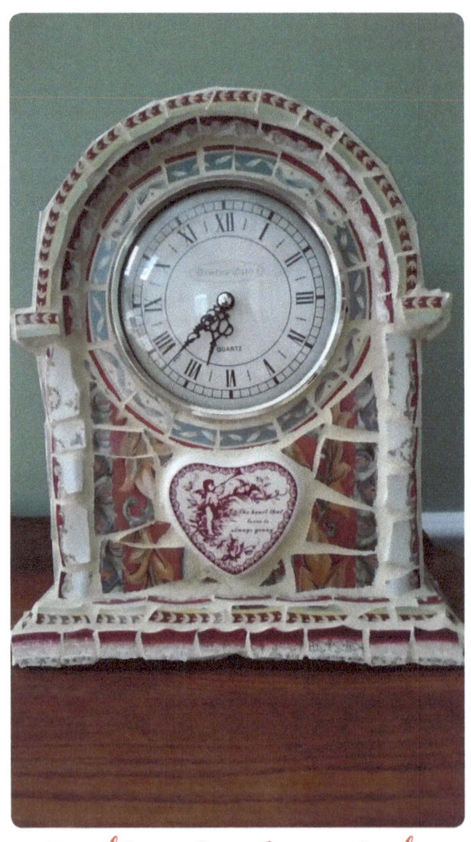

Jackie Spector Linder

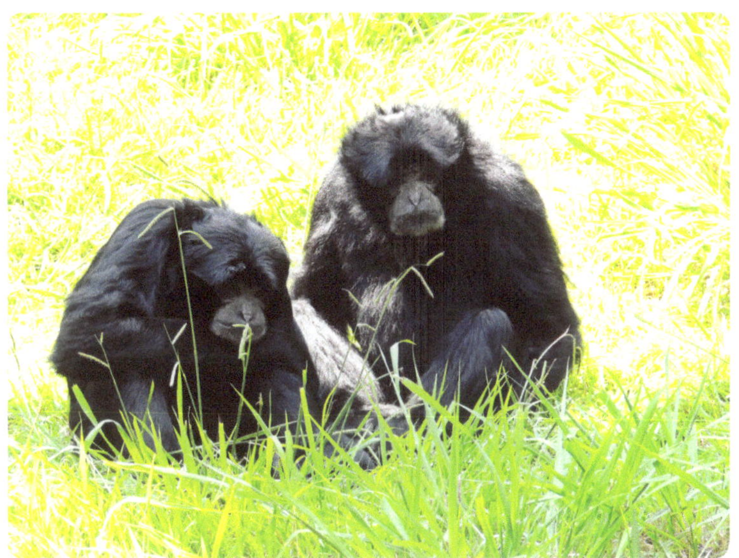

Traci Hallstrom

We sleep in separate rooms, we have dinner apart, we take separate vacations – we're doing everything we can to keep our marriage together.

- RODNEY DANGERFIELD (1921 – 2004)

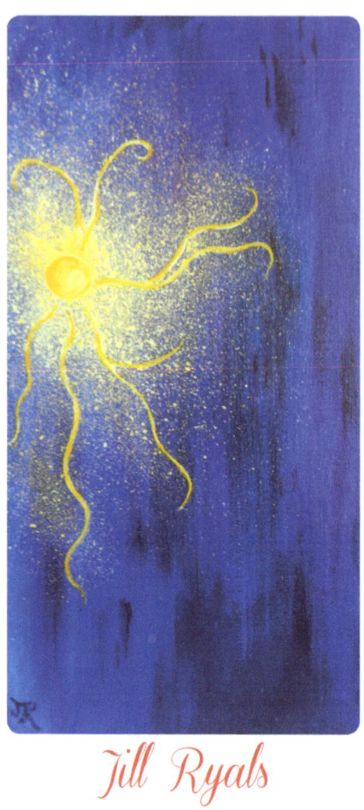

Jill Ryals

I wasn't always rich. There was a time I didn't know where my next husband was coming from.

- MAE WEST (1892 – 1980)

Paying alimony is like feeding hay to a dead horse.

- GROUCH MARX (1890 – 1977)

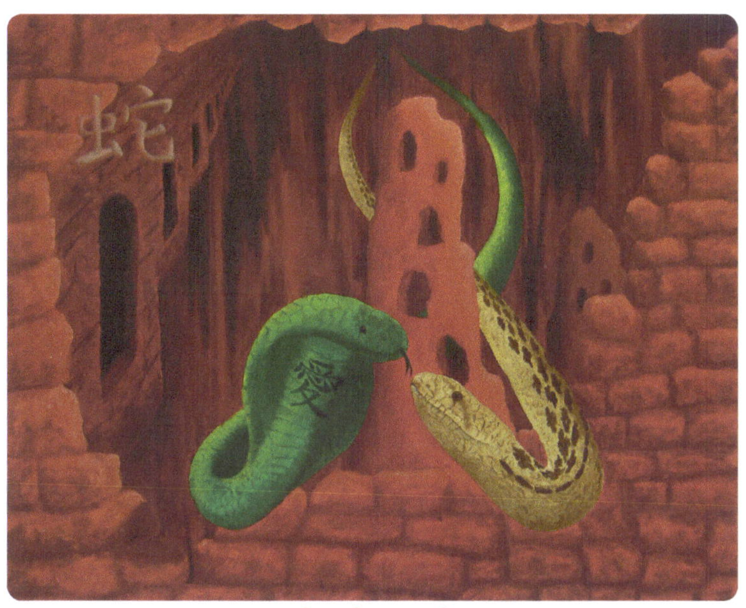

Lubosh Valenta

Brides aren't happy – they are just triumphant.

– JOHN BARRYMORE (1882 – 1942)

A man's friends like him but leave him as he is –
his wife loves him and is always trying
to turn him into somebody else.

- G.K. CHESTERTON (1874 – 1936)

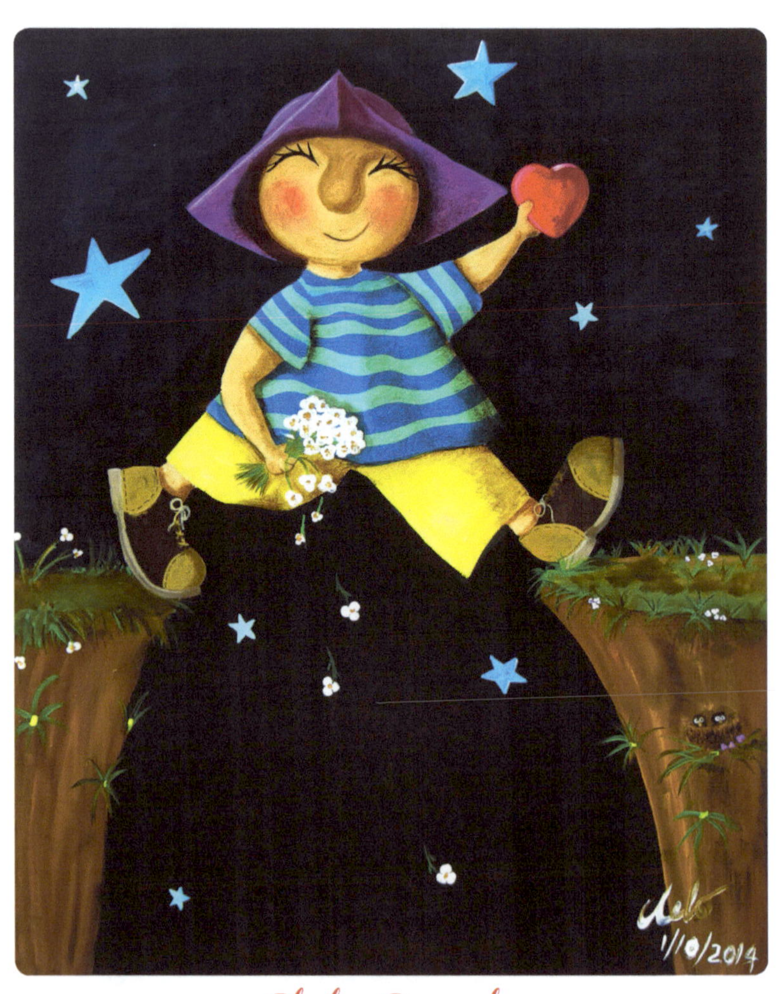

Chelo Gonzalez

Chapter 7

CHILDREN

Children today are tyrants.
They contradict their parents, gobble their food
and tyrannize their teachers.

- SOCRATES (470 – 399 BC)

My mother had a great deal of trouble with me,
but I think she enjoyed it.

- MARK TWAIN (1835 – 1910)

A child is a curly, dimpled lunatic.

- RALPH WALDO EMERSON (1803 – 1882)

Insanity is hereditary;
you can get it from your children.

SAM LEVENSON (1911 – 1980)

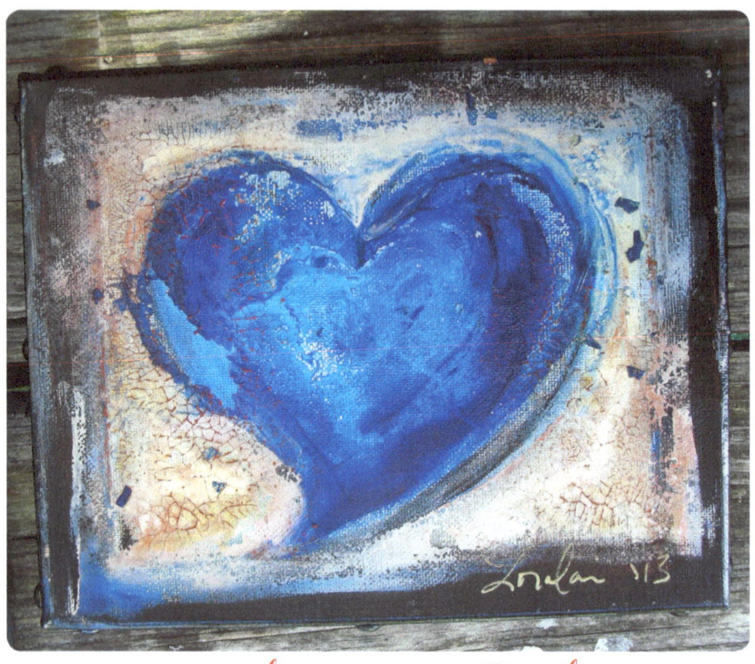

Loralai (Loryia Bond)

Insomnia: A contagious disease transmitted from babies to parents.

- IMMANUEL KANT (1724 – 1804)

Parents of young children should realize that few people, and maybe no one, will find their children as enchanting as they do.

- BARBARA WALTERS (1929 –)

Chapter 7
CHILDREN

Children are given us
to discourage our better emotions.

- HECTOR HUGH MUNRO "SAKI" (1870 – 1916)

Never have children, only grandchildren.

- GORE VIDAL (1925 – 2012)

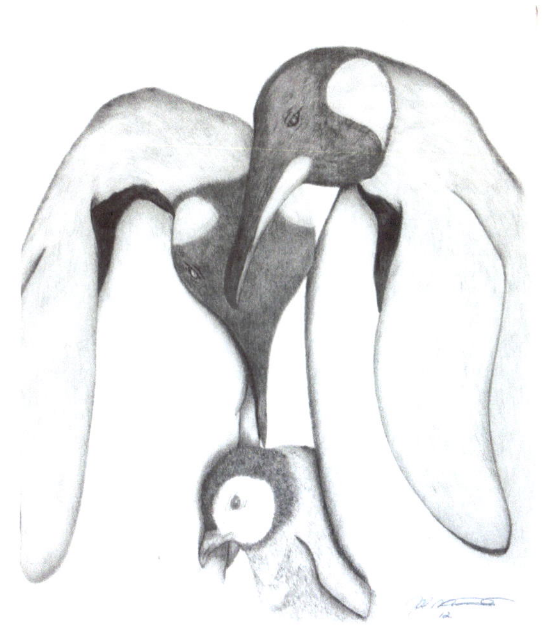

Jeff Montagne

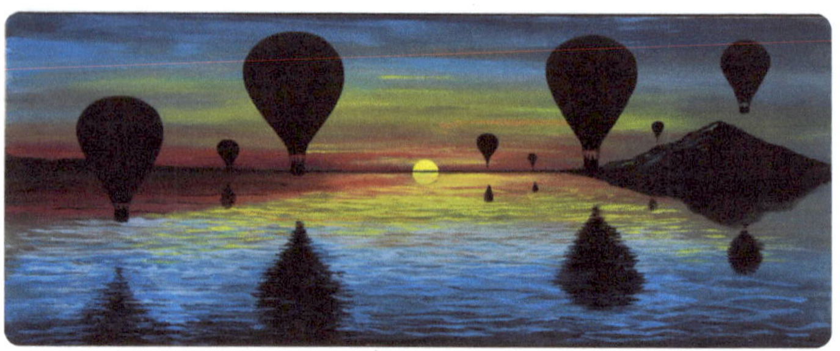

Dawn Hawkins

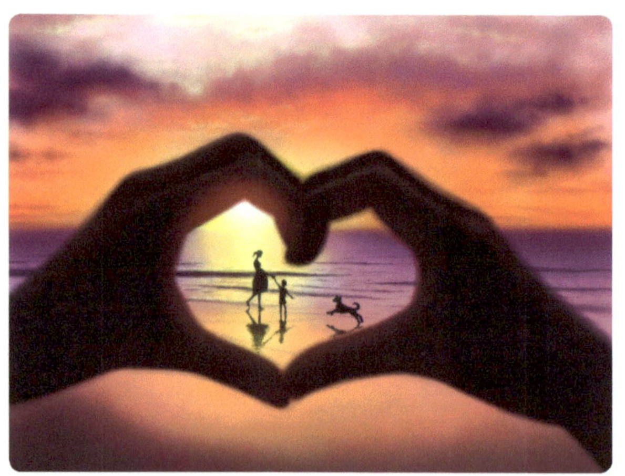

Mitzi Sato-Wiuff

When I was kidnapped, my parents snapped into action. They rented out my room.

- WOODY ALLEN (1935 –)

Chapter 7
CHILDREN

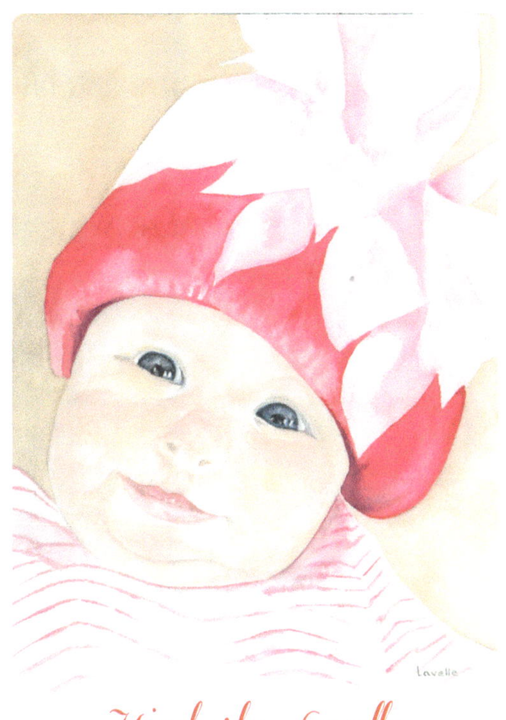

Kimberly Lavelle

All God's children are not beautiful. Most of God's children are, in fact, barely presentable.

- FRAN LEBOWITZ (1950 –)

We've been trying to have a kid. Well, she was trying, I just laid there.

- BOB SAGET (1956 –)

The thing that impresses me most about America is the way parents obey their children.

- DUKE OF WINDSOR (1894 – 1972)

When I was a boy of fourteen, my father was so ignorant I could hardly stand to have the old man around. But when I got to be 21, I was astonished at how much he had learned in seven years.

- MARK TWAIN (1835 – 1910)

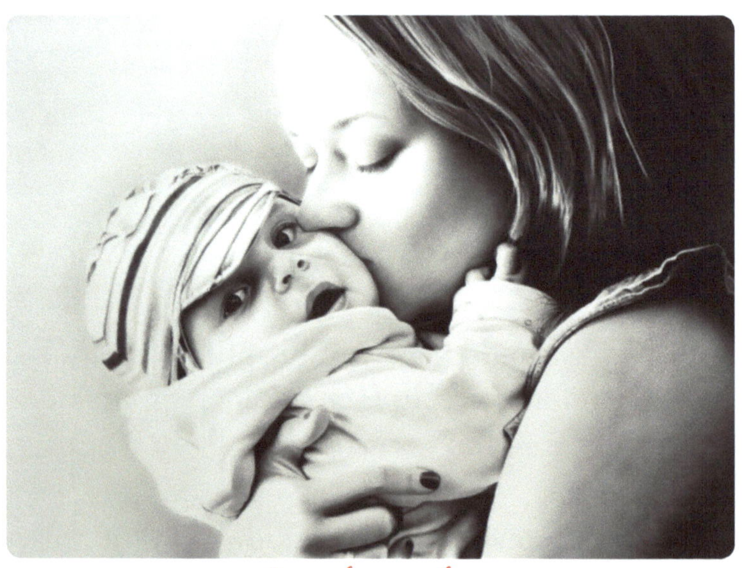

Ayush Mehra

Chapter 7
CHILDREN

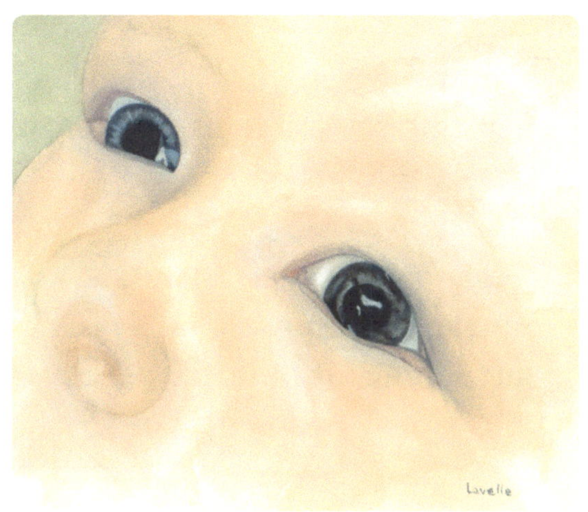

Kimberly Lavelle

Children make the most desirable opponents in Scrabble as they are both easy to beat and fun to cheat.

- FRAN LEBOWITZ (1950 –)

A baby is an inestimable blessing and a bother.

- MARK TWAIN (1835 – 1916)

A happy childhood is poor preparation for human contact.

- COLETTE (1873 – 1954)

No matter how old a mother is, she watches her middle-aged children for signs of improvement.

- FLORIDA SCOTT-MAXWELL (1883 – 1979)

The best way to keep children at home
is to make the atmosphere pleasant –
and let the air out of the tires.

- DOROTHY PARKER (1893 – 1967)

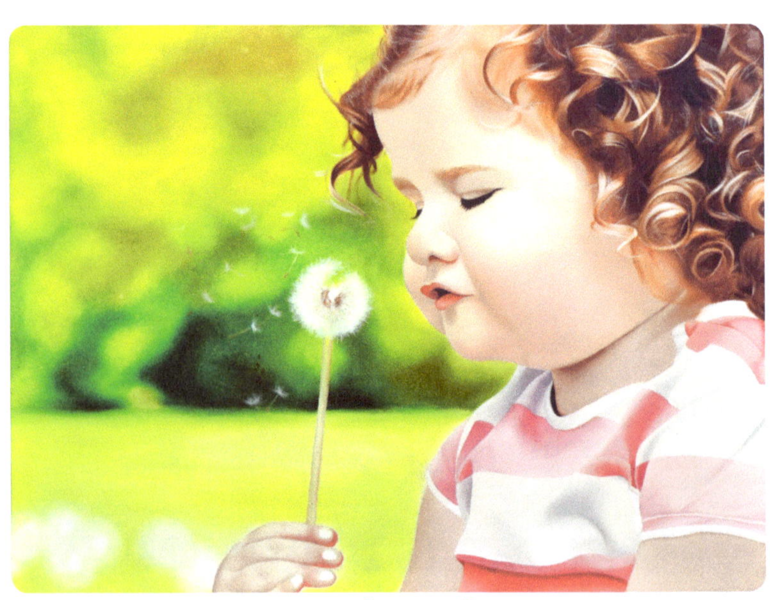

Ayush Mehra

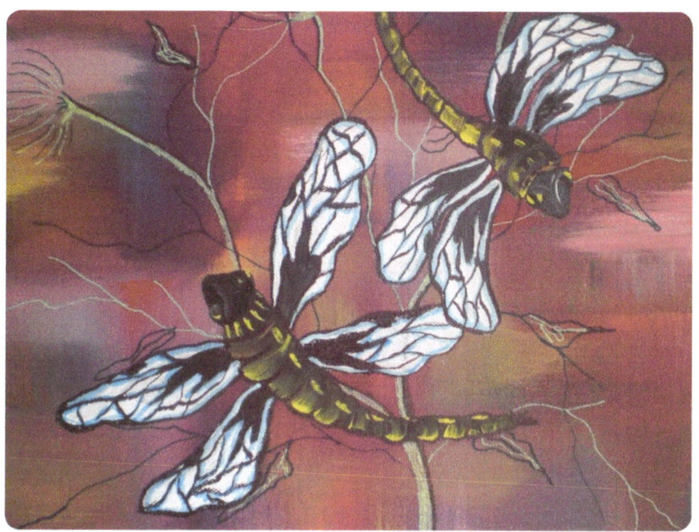

Dawn Hawkins

I'm for bringing back the birch,
but only for consenting adults.

- GORE VIDAL (1925 – 2012)

It is no wonder that people are so horrible
when they start life as children.

- KINGSLEY AMIS (1922 – 1995)

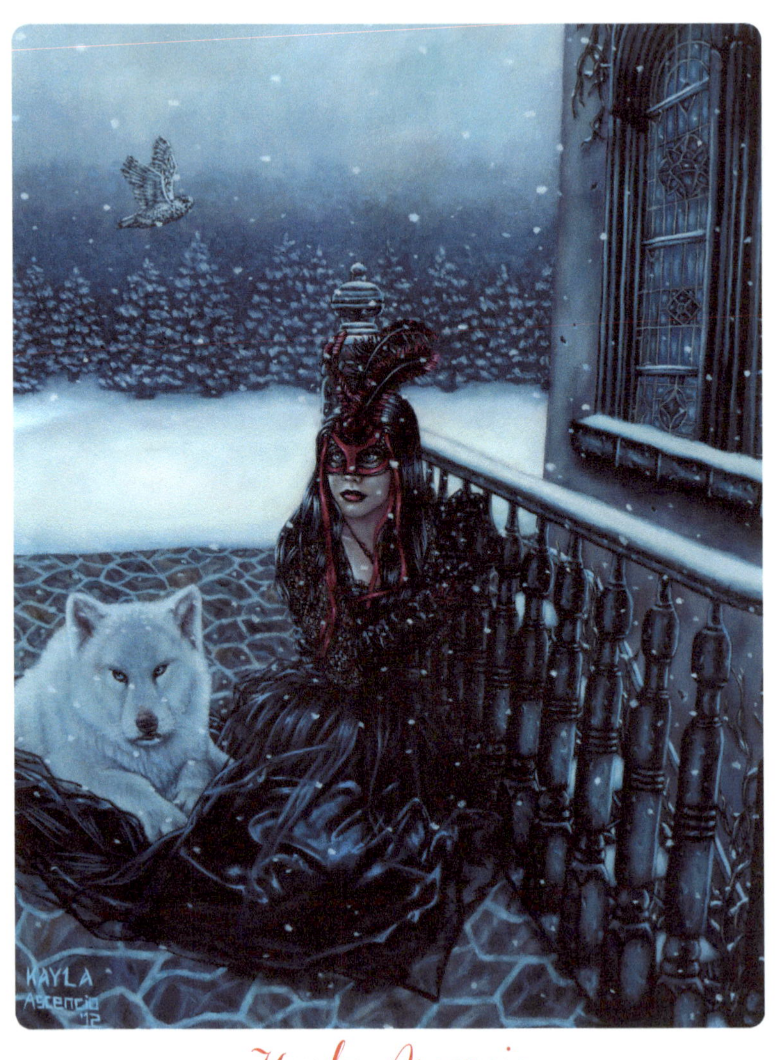

Kayla Ascencio

Chapter 8

FURRY FRIENDS

Until one has loved an animal,
a part of one's soul remains unawakened.

- ANATOLE FRANCE (1844 – 1924)

Dogs are the most amazing creatures;
they give unconditional love.
For me they are the role model for being alive.

- GILDA RADNER (1946 – 1989)

The only creatures that are evolved enough to
convey pure love are dogs and infants.

- JOHNNY DEPP (1963 –)

Buy a pup and your money will buy love unflinching.

– RUDYARD KIPLING (1865 – 1936)

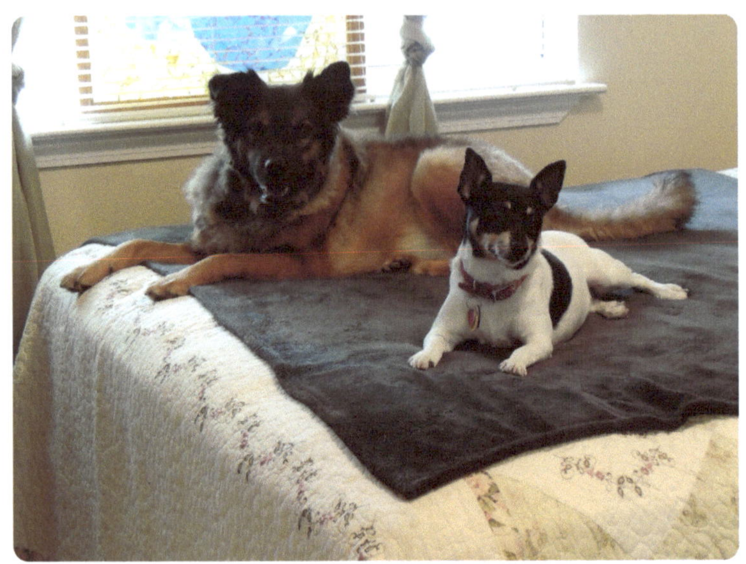

Traci Hallstrom

Man himself cannot express love and humility by external signs, so plainly as does a dog, when with dropping ears, hanging lips, flexuous body, and wagging tail, he meets his beloved master.

- CHARLES DARWIN (1809 – 1882)

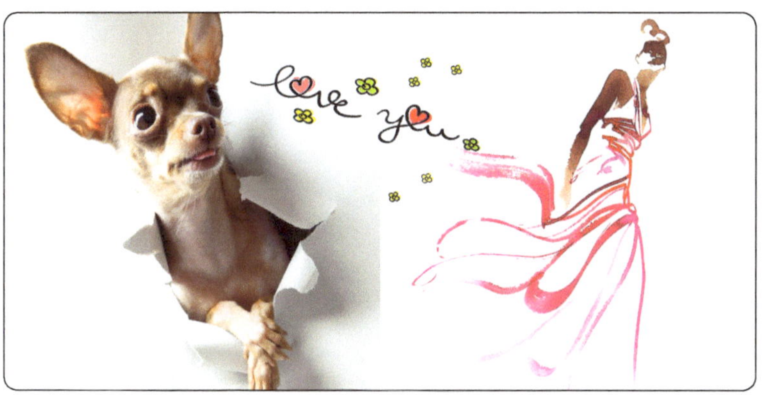

Aida Novosel

Dog! When we first met on the highway of life,
we came from the two poles of creation...
What can be the meaning of the obscure love
for me that has sprung up in your heart?

- ANATOLE FRANCE (1844 – 1924)

The bond with a true dog is as lasting as the ties
of this earth can ever be.

- KONRAD A. LORENZ (1903 – 1989)

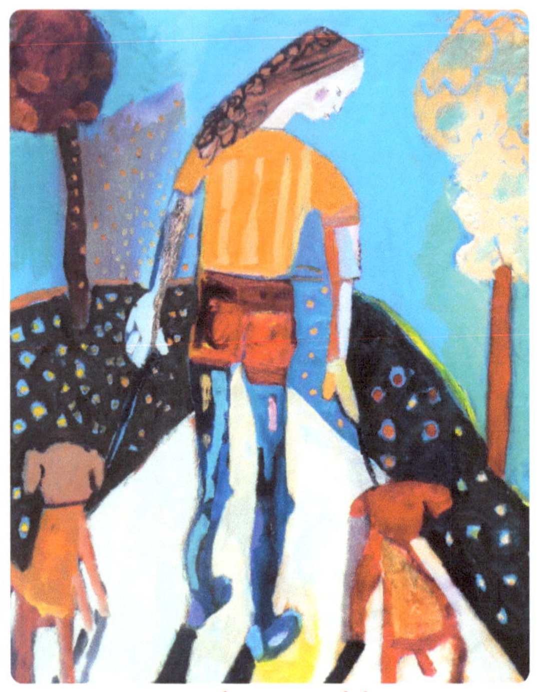

Carolyn Schlam

Blessed is the person who has earned the love of an old dog.

- SIDNEY JEANNE SEWARD (1922 –)

The poor dog, in life the firmest friend, The first to welcome, foremost to defend.

- LORD BYRON (1788 – 1824)

To many, the words love, hope,
and dreams are synonymous with horses.

- OLIVER WENDELL HOLMES, SR. (1809 – 1894)

A good man will take care of his horses and dogs, not only while they are young, but also when they are old and past service.

- PLUTARCH (46 – 120)

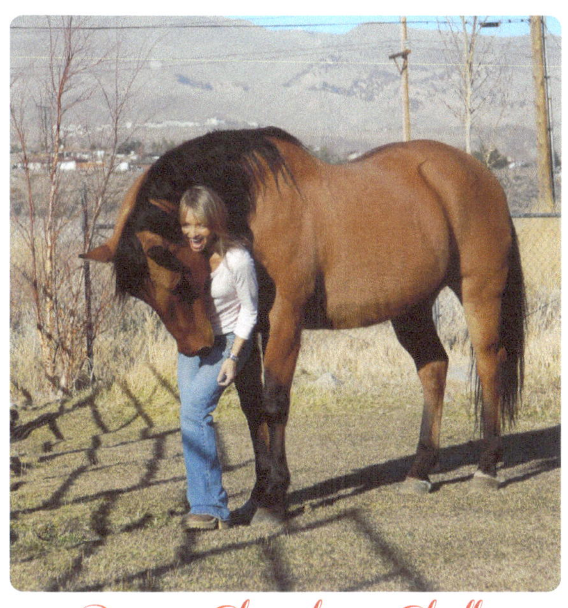

Renee Chambers Cholla

A chieftain was challenged to a duel by an enemy and killed, and when his adversary came to strip his body of his armor, his horse kicked him and bit him till he died.

- PLINY THE ELDER (23 – 79)

He doth nothing but talk of his horse.

- WILLIAM SHAKESPEARE (1564 – 1616)

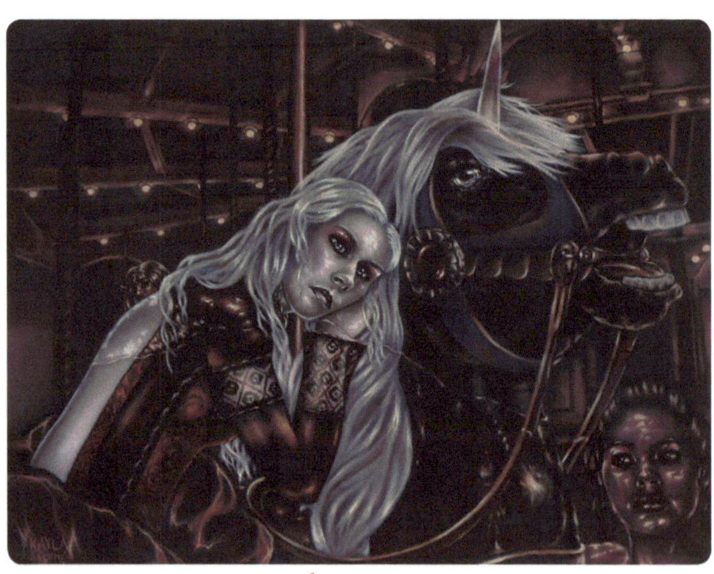

Kayla Ascencio

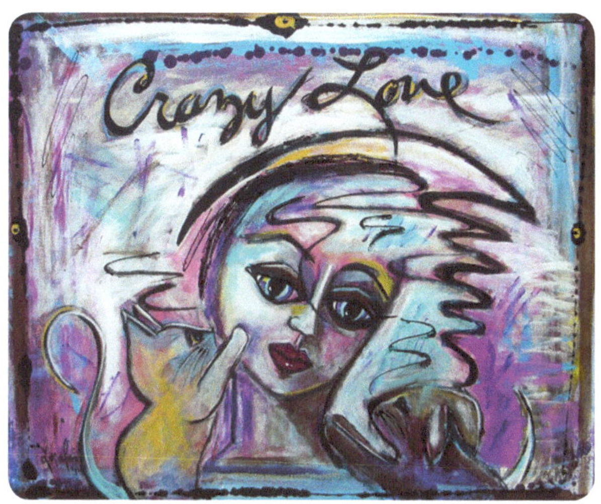

Loralai (Loryia Bond)

Cats do not declare their love much; they enact it, by their myriad invocations of our pleasure.

- VICKI HEARNE (1946 – 2001)

The smallest feline is a masterpiece.

- LEONARDO DA VINCI (1452 – 1519)

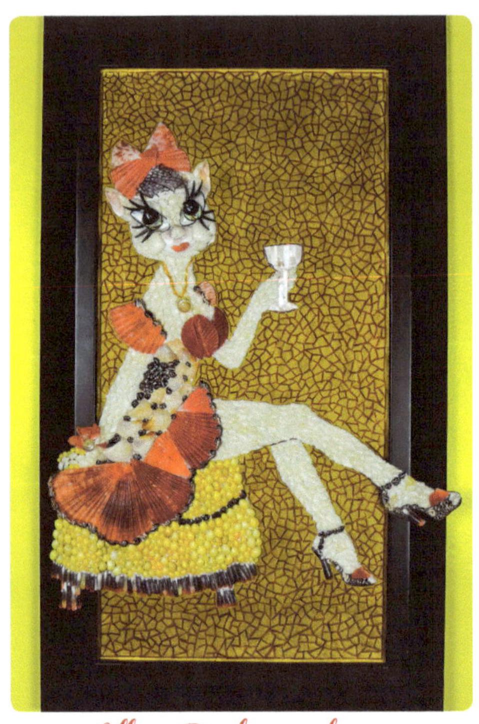

Alla Baksanskaya

I love cats because I enjoy my home;
and little by little, they become its visible soul.

- JEAN COCTEAU (1889 – 1963)

There is not a man living who knows better than I that the four charms of a cat lie in its closed eyes, its long and lovely hair, its silence, and even its affected love.

- HILAIRE BELLOC (1870 – 1953)

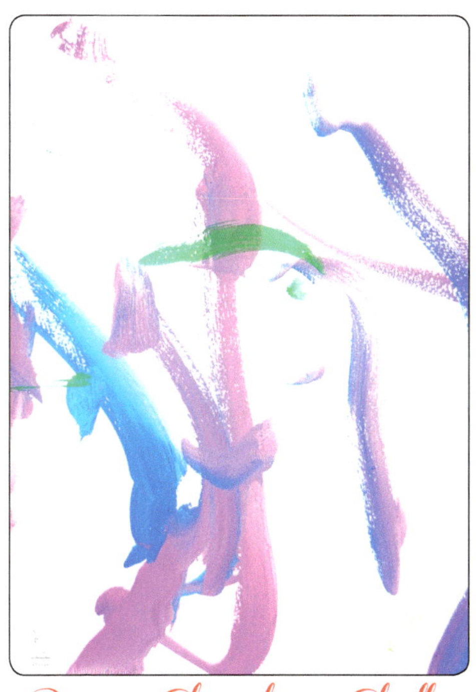

Renee Chambers Cholla

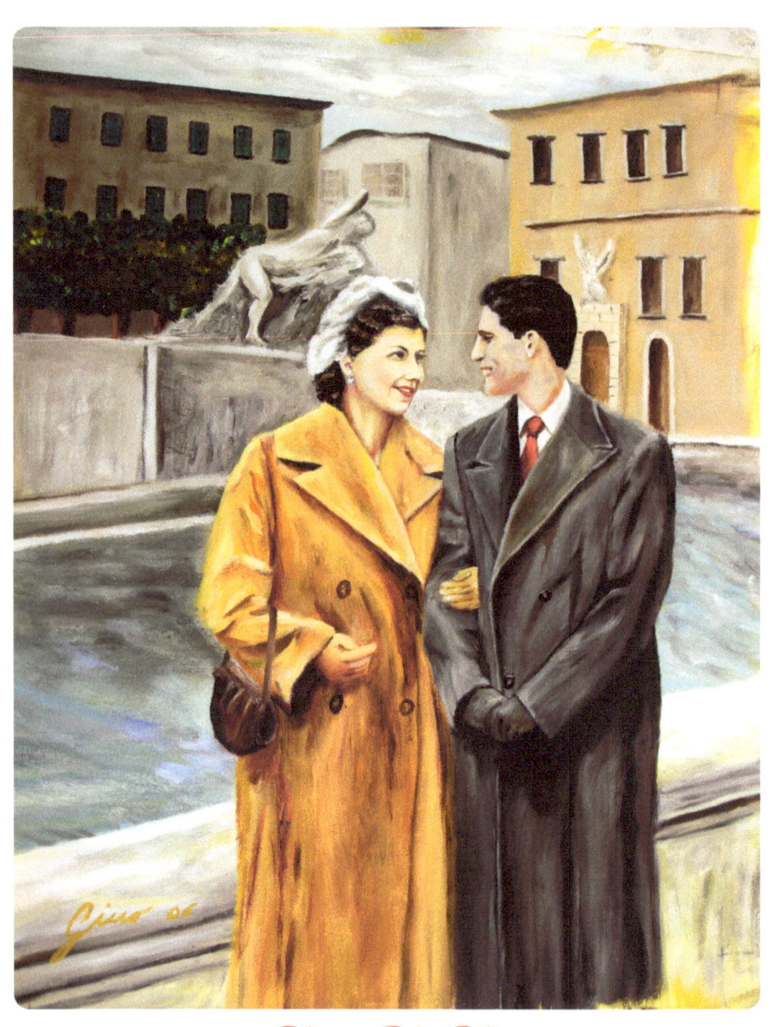

Gino Di Dio

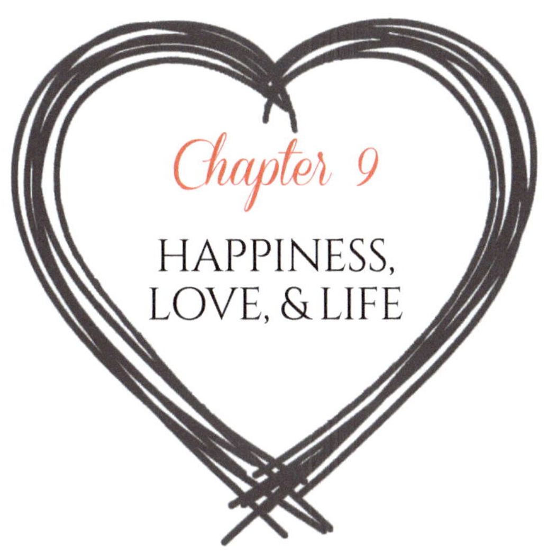

The good life is one inspired by love
and guided by knowledge.

- BERTRAND RUSSELL (1872 – 1970)

The longer I live, the more beautiful life becomes.

- FRANK LLOYD WRIGHT (1867 – 1959)

Grief can take care of itself;
but to get the full value of a joy,
you must have somebody to divide it with.

- MARK TWAIN (1835 – 1910)

Happy is he who causes scandal.

- SALVADOR DALI (1904 – 1989)

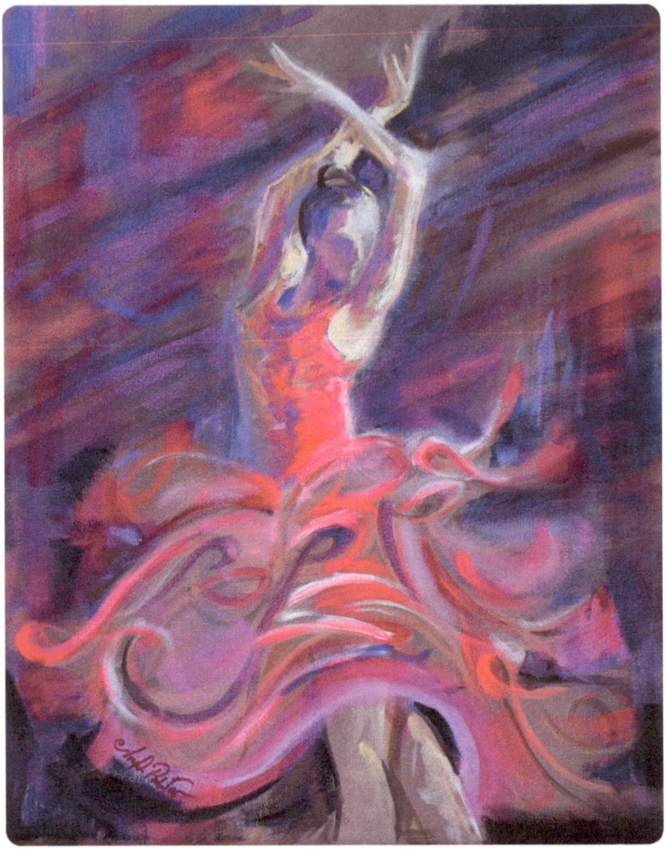

Joseph Palotas

The trouble with life is that there are so many beautiful women and so little time.

- JOHN BARRYMORE (1882 – 1942)

The secret of being miserable is to have the leisure to bother about whether you are happy or not.

- GEORGE BERNARD SHAW (1856 – 1950)

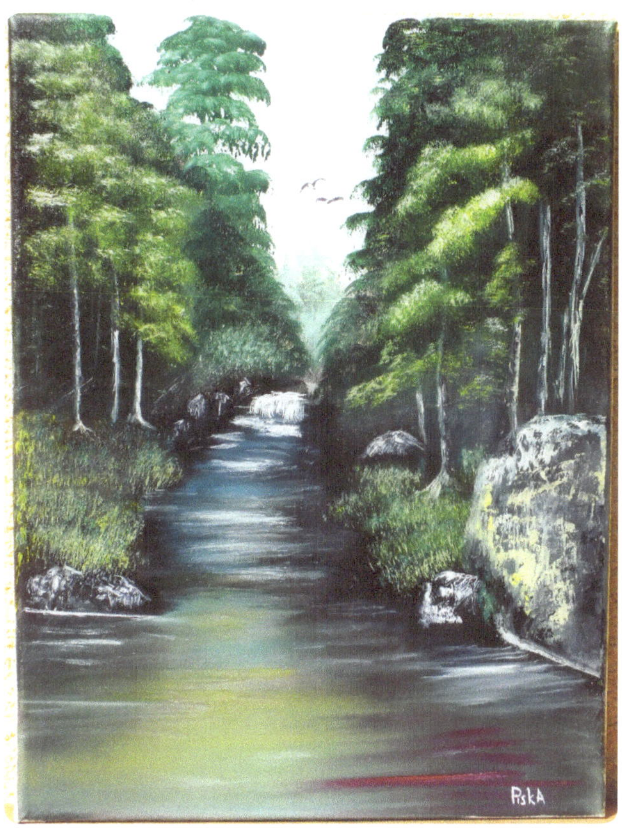

Beata Piska

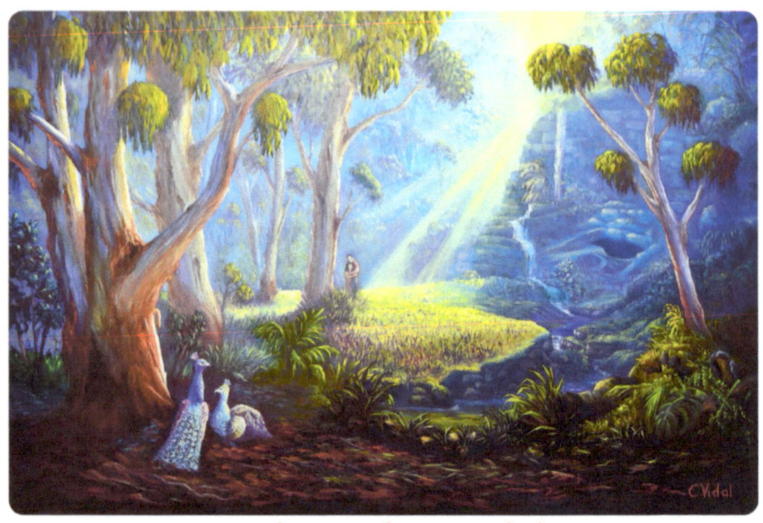

Christopher Vidal

The greater part of our happiness
or misery depends on our dispositions
and not on our circumstances.

- MARTHA WASHINGTON (1731 – 1802)

If only we'd stop trying to be happy,
we could have a pretty good time.

- EDITH WHARTON (1862 – 1937)

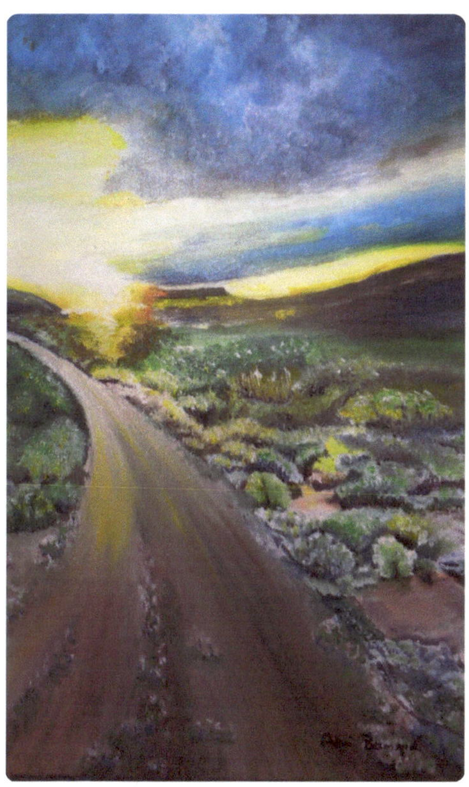

Adri Barnard

It is neither wealth nor splendor, but tranquility and occupation which give happiness.

- THOMAS JEFFERSON (1743 – 1826)

**Life would be infinitely happier
if we could only be born at the age of eighty
and gradually approach eighteen.**

MARK TWAIN (1835 – 1910)

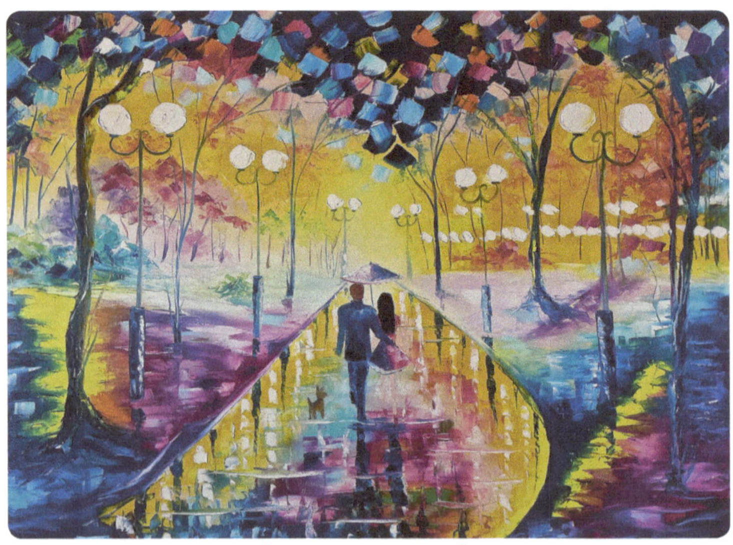

Eleonora Pulcini

We must laugh at man to avoid crying for him.

- NAPOLEON BONAPARTE (1769 – 1821)

To be stupid, selfish and have good health are three requirements for happiness.

- GUSTAVE FLAUBERT (1821 – 1880)

The unexamined life is not worth living.

- SOCRATES (470 – 399 BC)

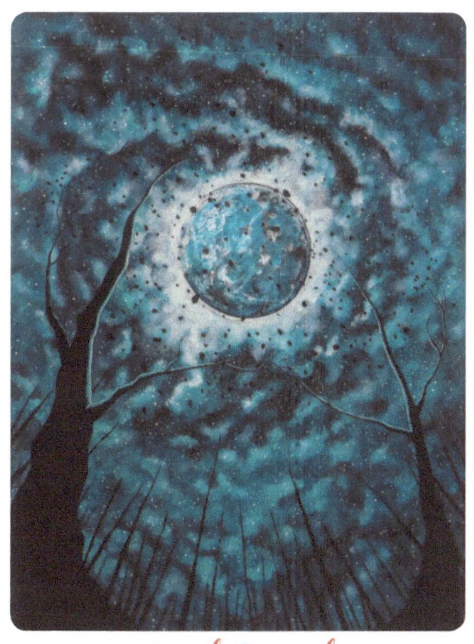

Joel Tesch

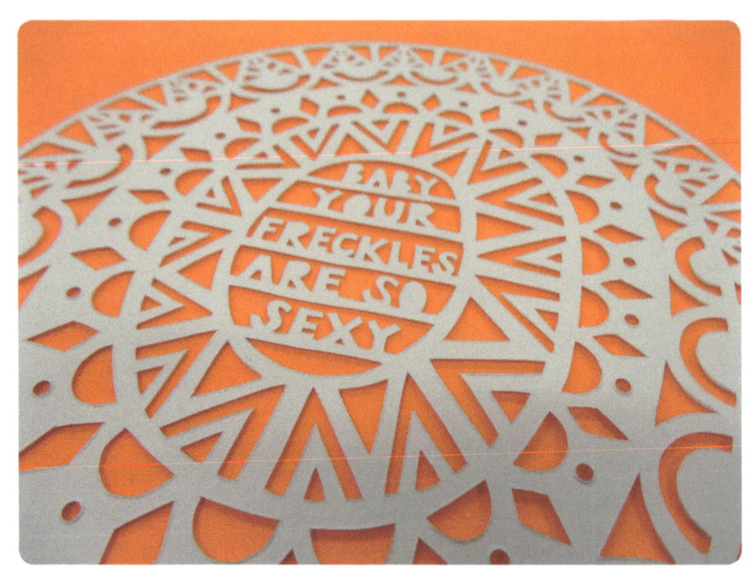

Ellen Schlobohm

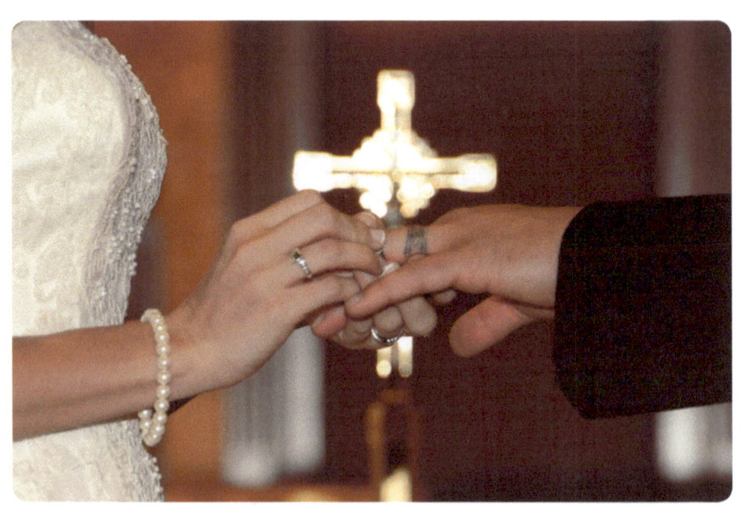

Earl Devendorf

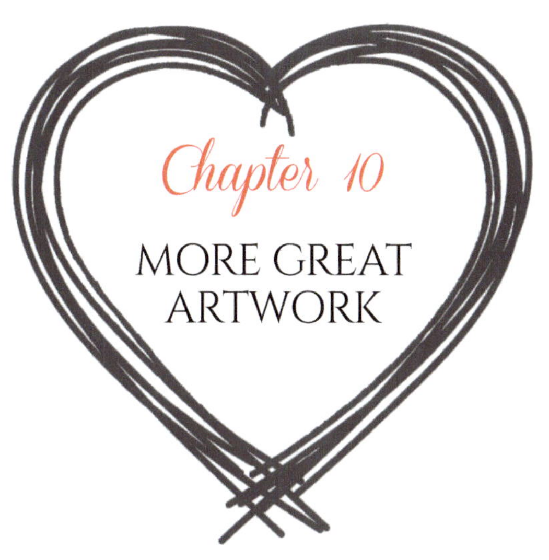

Chapter 10

MORE GREAT ARTWORK

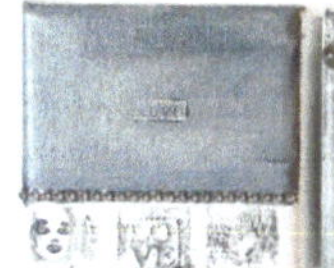
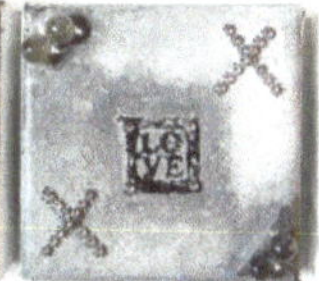

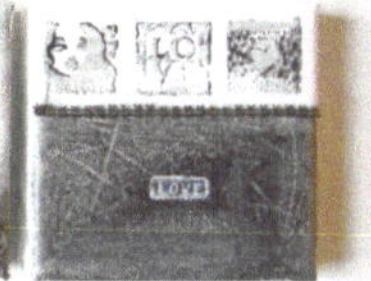

Christine Marshall

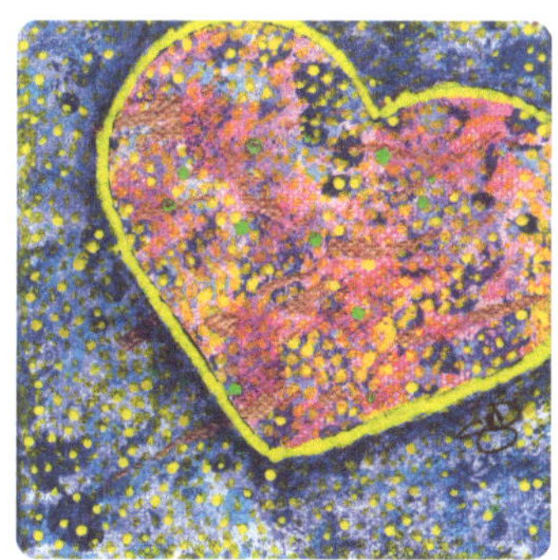

Sheila Delgado

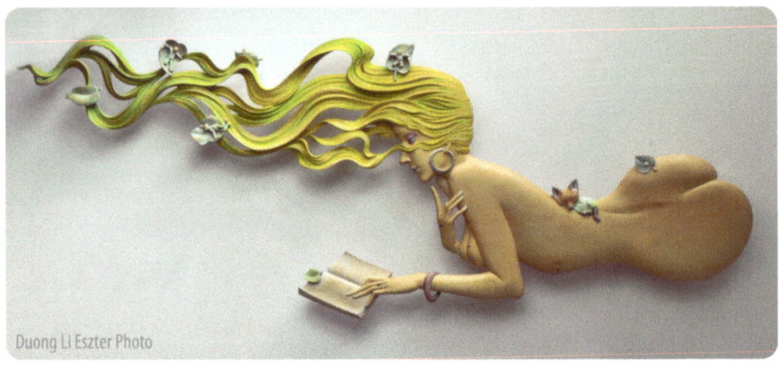

Ferenc Somogyi

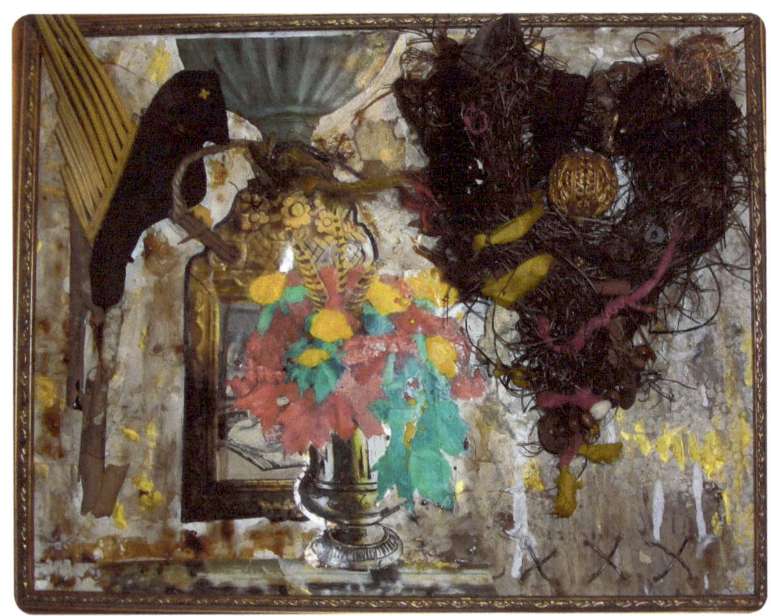

Melissa Bruneau

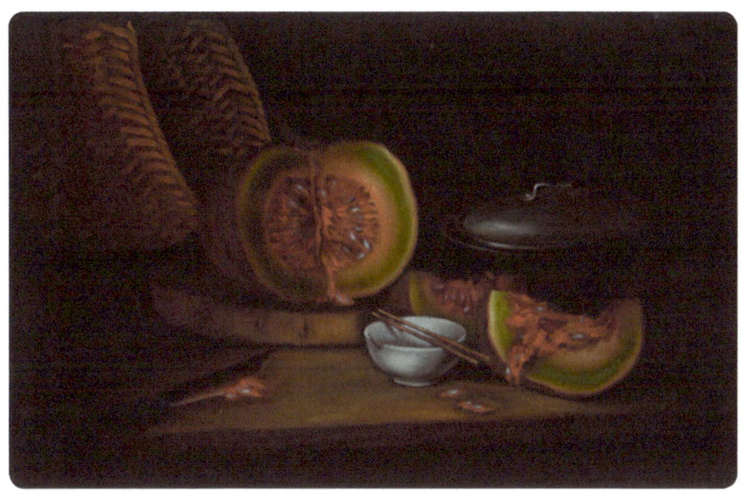

Ninh Le

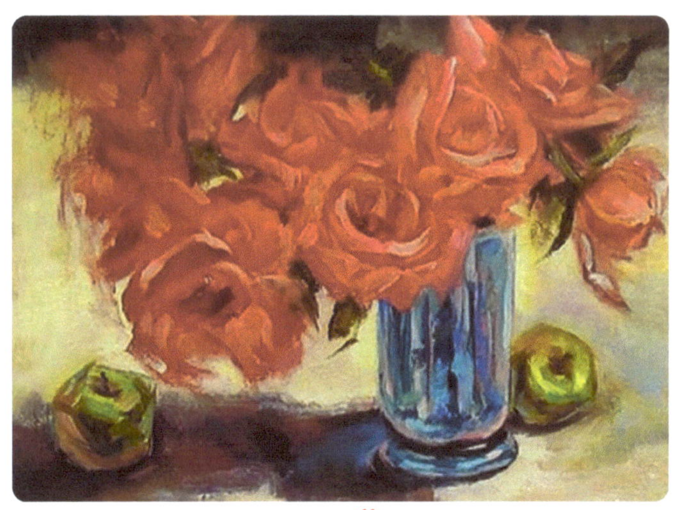

Patricia Elliott Seitz

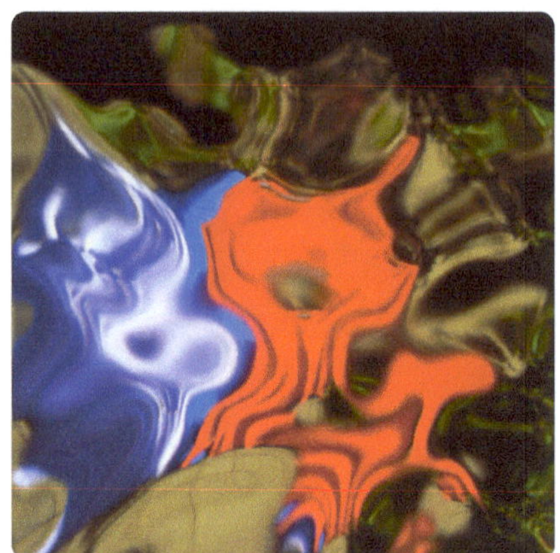

Carlos de Jong

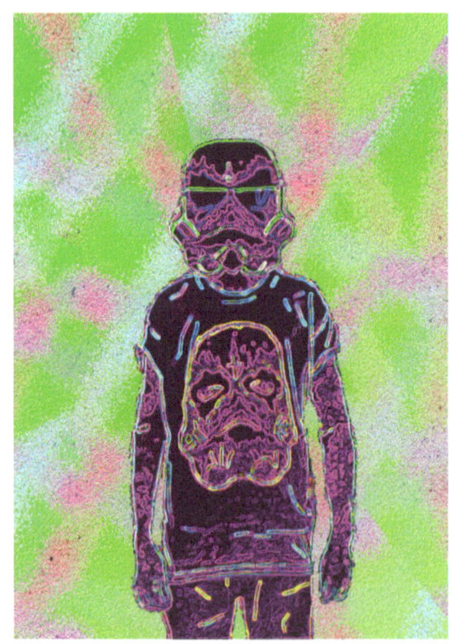

Jimmy Morales

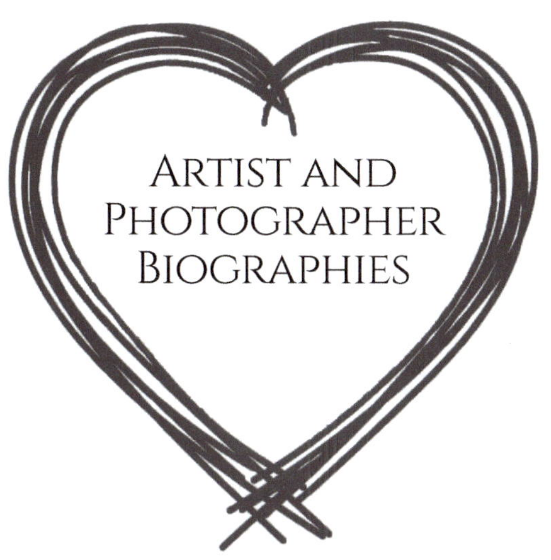

ARTIST AND PHOTOGRAPHER BIOGRAPHIES

KAYLA ASCENCIO - PAGES 13, 56, 66, 71, 88, 94

Kayla was born in a small town located in southwestern Pennsylvania in 1988. She received an Associate in Specialized Business Degree for the illustration program at Douglas Education Center. Kayla's first love is fantasy art. She also enjoys painting animals and portraits. Kayla lives in southwestern Pennsylvania and is currently taking commissions. View her work on her website at www.kaylafantasyart.com or visit her Facebook page "Kayla Ascencio Fantasy Art" or on Deviantart www.ascenciok.deviantart.com. Contact her at ascenciok@yahoo.com.

KATRINA AVOTINA - PAGES 12, 31, 59

Katrina came from Latvia where her family had several generations of artists. She has been exhibiting since the age of 16 and has won several awards. She now lives in the city of Leeds, West Yorkshire, UK. See more of her artwork and contact her on her website www.katrinaavotina.com and through Facebook at www.Facebook.com/KatrinaAvotinaPaintings.

ALLA BAKSANSKAYA - PAGES 44, 60, 96

Alla is an award-winning artist working with natural seashells. She uses colorful seashells and acrylic paint to create her unique three-dimensional works of art. She creates mosaic, collages, figurines and other decorative items. All are one-of-a-kind items. Alla's style is modern, from abstract flowers to portraits, from mosaics to acrylic or oil paintings and from diptychs to art collages.

Alla won numerous awards at prestigious Sanibel Island, FL, and Philadelphia seashell shows in 2009 and 2010. Since 1994 Alla has lived in New York City with her family. It is here where she has started to create art full-time.

Visit her website www.allaexpression.com or on Facebook at Alla Baksanskaya.

ADRI BARNARD - PAGES 36, 38, 103

Adri was born in Vredenburg, South Africa. She matriculated at Volkskool, Potchefstroom. Adri has hosted several art exhibitions and her own gallery. View her work on Facebook at: Adri Barnard oil paintings. Contact her by email at: barnard.adri@gmail.com or by phone at: 072 848 9044.

MELISSA BRUNEAU - PAGES 50, 108

"Raised in Baltimore, Maryland, Melissa grew up as an adventurous, courageous risk taker, resourceful and fearless. Characteristics like those helped build not only her background, but inspiration as well. Not often expressing herself outwardly, she worked through her art to begin a therapy of getting it all out on canvas. After studying Fine Art at The Community College of Baltimore County, she later relocated in Tampa to continue her love and education for art. Melissa attended The International Academy of Design and Technology, majoring in Interior Design. Developing a desire for balance, order, value and dimension in her life, she can now fulfill her passion not

only as a full-time artist but as a professional organizer. Still pursuing the depths of her soul. Her art is an interpretation of perspective, orchestrated with objects that have come into her life by chance, randomly, or hold a sentimental meaning. Each and every creation of her collection is conceived and created with great emotion and passion. Some of her creations are conceived through times of heavy burdens or great heartache, while others display Melissa's love for life and all things that are fun and beautiful in this wonderful world. Many of her works of art have hidden visual messages or repetitive themes embedded within them that speak to a deep personal side of her own emotions."

Thank you again for your support of the arts and Melissa's personal collection of work. You may follow her exhibits on Facebook at http://www.facebook.com/Melissas MixedMediaArt or contact her at redledhead@yahoo.com.

CHOLLA CHAMBERS (RENEE CHAMBERS) - PAGES 93, 97

Cholla Chambers is a horse and an international artist. He has won two honorable mention Art Awards, one from Venice, Italy, where he was also given a solo show in 2009. His art has shown in galleries across the USA including NYC, Vegas, Reno, and San Francisco. His art has been described as having "the fire of Pollock" and "the fixed gaze of Resnick." Yes, he is a horse. His very proud owner is Renee Chambers. You can learn more about Cholla and his art at www.ArtistIsaHorse.com.

IONE CITRIN - PAGES 11, 21

Ione's art has shown nationally since 1998 when, after years of world travel, a successful television, radio, theater and film career in the performing arts, she decided to focus her richly diverse talents on the visual arts. Ione's artistic expression, creativity, and passion for communication have resulted in numerous awards for her painting, sculpture, mixed media, and assemblage. Her work has also been featured in several important publications. Ione maintains an extensive exhibition schedule in juried, non-juried, and invitational arts venues. Contact her at: Ione Citrin, 2222 Avenue of the Stars, Suite 2302, Los Angeles CA 90067; phone: (310) 556-4382; www.artbyione.com; ICitrin@aol.com.

SHEILA DELGADO - PAGES 24, 107

Sheila studied graphic design and computer graphic arts, but is mainly a self-taught artist. While watercolor is often her first choice, she works equally in acrylic, mixed media, digital art, fabric and surface design. She finds inspiration in the Southern California landscape, from the flourishing coast, to the barren high desert. You are welcome to contact her at shemar67@gmail.com, or via her website.

Website and Blog: http://www.sheiladelgado.com/
Facebook: https://www.Facebook.com/sheila.delgado.10
Zazzle shop: http://www.zazzle.com/sheilascorner
Spoonflower shop:
http://www.spoonflower.com/profiles/demouse
LinkedIn:
http://www.linkedin.com/pub/sheila-delgado/30/380/280
Pinterest: http://www.pinterest.com/sheilartist/

EARL DEVENDORF - PAGES 64, 106

Earl is a professional photographer from Carbondale PA. He enjoys photographing a wide range of subjects.

View his work on Facebook at: https://www.Facebook.com/earl.devendorf or contact him at: earldevendorf@yahoo.com.

GINO DI DIO - PAGES 14, 63, 98

Gino is a professional artist who specializes in oil paintings on not only canvas but also natural materials such as slate, stone and terra cotta. Gino's artistic technique comes from the inspirations of his native land, Naples, Italy. He captures the beauty of people in oil portraits, cultures in murals, and brings landscapes to life. Gino's studio is located in Damascus, VA.

Gino is a juried member with work on exhibit at *Heartwood, Southwest Virginia's Artisan Gateway, Arts Depot,* Abingdon, VA, the *Crescent Moon*, Wilmington, NC, *Trails ART Ware*, Damascus, VA, and Round the Mountain, Southwest Virginia's Artisan Network. His murals can also be viewed in the Damascus, VA Town Park.

He has studied at Florence Art School, NYU, and Virginia Museum of Fine Arts in Richmond. His portfolio of paintings and contact information is available at www.ginosart.com and www.Facebook.com/oilpaintingsbygino. Email at gdidio56@yahoo.com.

SUE GARDNER - PAGE 73

Sue is based near Ashby de la Zouch, England, in the National Forest. She likes to use very vibrant color combinations in her work. Her subjects are chosen for the way they catch the light in an interesting and often beautiful way. Her work can be seen on her website www.sue-gardner-art.com and at Whitepeaks Fine Art in London. Her Facebook page is https://www.Facebook.com/SueGardnerArt and she has a daily blog here http://sue-gardner-art.blogspot.co.uk/.

LESLEY GILES - PAGES 20, 23, 33, 46

Lesley is an internationally collected artist from England. She lived and painted in London most of her life until she moved to Florida in 2003 with her American husband to follow his career. They

relocated to the Eastern Shore, MD in 2012 where she paints in her studio overlooking the wild Choptank River.

Lesley is primarily a landscape painter inspired by solitary places and isolated objects which was why her husband (an avid golfer) could see a potential for her to paint GOLF COURSES—very strange landscapes! She paints with oil, watercolor and pastel; vital to her work is a strong and theatrical light. In 1999 she was selected to be the **Tournament Artist** for the **Ladies European Tour** which involved traveling with the tour and exhibiting her paintings at different clubhouses along with painting commissions that were used as tournament prizes. The most memorable tournaments were the Laura Davies Invitational at Brocket Hall, **England**, the Rover European Cup at Praia D'El Rey, **Portugal**, which pitted the Men's European Seniors v the Ladies and the very evocative Marrakech Palmeraie Open in **Morocco**.

Lesley is a graduate of Goldsmiths' College, BFA, and the Royal College of Art, MFA, London. She has exhibited extensively in galleries and museums in the UK, Europe, the USA and also in China following a Visiting Painter invitation to Urumqi, Xinjiang, in 1996. Lesley has had solo shows in London, Florida, France and China. Her work has been published by Harper Collins in "Watercolour Masterclass" and "The Challenge of Landscape" as well as being featured in several magazines.

Her paintings are collected all over the world and they can be found in private and museum collections in the United Kingdom, the United States, France, China and Australia.

"… The boldness of her colour is matched by a strength of design that is all too rare in contemporary art. Here is an artist with a down-to-earth sureness of vision that is immensely beguiling"—**Andrew Lambirth**, Art Writer, *Spectator Magazine*, London, 2006

Lesley's website www.lesleygilesart.com

Email: lesleygilesart@aol.com

Facebook Page: https://www.Facebook.com/lesley.giles.12

JESSE GLENN - PAGE 40

Jesse lives and works in Berea, KY. He is a professional visual artist and art instructor. His artwork has an illustrative quality to it, conveying emotion and depth with bold hues, hard lines and vivid detail. He uses vibrant colors and energetic shapes to express beauty and meaning with a modern, contemporary style. His work is representational yet non-realistic, true to form with a distinctive view. Jesse says, "I paint life as I see and feel it in a way that deviates from normality." View his work on his website www.jglennmodernart.webs.com or on Facebook at www.facebook.com/jglennmodernart.

CHELO GONZALEZ - PAGES 6, 55, 78

Chelo is a very talented and gifted artist. His paintings are unique and have a whimsical quality. Here is a collection of his most recent works. They are three-dimensional mixed media paintings. He also does portraits.

Chelo's studio is located in Ajijic and Tlaquepaque, Jalisco, Mexico. For commission work please contact him through Facebook Chelo's "gordas" oil paintings or www.chelogonzalez.com or janiemunoz9@hotmail.com or by phone to 331 527 9347.

TRACI HALLSTROM - PAGES 75, 90

Traci found her love for ceramic mosaic art almost by accident when she enrolled in a class she thought was on stained glass art but was in fact a ceramics class. She never looked back. You can view her at the following locations: www.fluffypuppiesmosaics.com, www.flickr.com/photos/fluffypuppiesmosaics, www.etsy.com/shop/FluffyPuppiesMosaic and www.twitter.com/mosaicstones, or on her Facebook page "Fluffy Puppies Mosaics Art." Contact Traci at Traci.Hallstrom@gmail.com or by phone at 530-339-0210.

DAWN HAWKINS - PAGES 82, 87

Dawn's passion from childhood has always been drawing and painting. At the age of 15, her family settled in Knoxville, TN. She works with numerous mediums, but is most comfortable and passionate about acrylics and watercolors. Her artwork includes fine art on canvas, wood, slate, and tile and large-scale murals in private homes and businesses. She has an obsession with painting dragonflies which have become her signature in a sense, their grace and beauty is amazing, one to be shared with the world.

She is an artist at The Gallery Nuance at 121 S. Gay St. You can also find her work at The Earth To The Old City, Stillhouse Tavern, Green Earth Emporium, The Artist Village, Ijams nature center, Mulligans, Dragonfly Art Dimensions in Gatlinburg, Union County Arts, and Cumberland Ridge Primitives.

Her website is ThruTheLookingGlassMurals.com
Her Facebook page is
https://www.Facebook.com/pages/Dawn-Hawkins-Artist/204753446282882?ref=bookmarks
Email her at hawki4@hotmail.com

KATE HUNTINGTON - PAGES 8, 25

Kate is a Rhode Island School of Design alumna, and has been working as a representational painter based in Providence, RI, continuously since 1976. Her work has been shown in and about New England in galleries and museums and featured in several distinguished books. Her paintings and drawings are found in numerous national and international private and corporate collections and have been featured in a number of TV shows and movies as well. She is a member of the Copley Society in Boston. You can see more of her work on Facebook at Kate Huntington Oil Paintings. Her contact info is katesstudios@yahoo.com.

CARLOS DE JONG - PAGES 43, 110

Carlos, in addition to being an artist, is an architect and urban planner. As an artist, he has been developing his art production during the last seven years, independently of his professional work as an architect and planner, around the world. His working trips to North Africa and the Middle East, especially the Persian Gulf and Mesopotamia, awakened his creativity. He found a need to search forms related to the genesis of life and the evolution of the universe and the creative process. In 2012, Carlos as an artist started his own professional art activity. Currently, he is launching his artwork from Mendoza, Argentina, to worldwide potential collectors.

His contact information is:
Carlos de Jong – Wokshop and Art Gallery
Pasteur 1001, CP 5519, Guaymallén, Mendoza, Argentina
Email: charly1584@gmail.com – cdejong@speedy.com.ar
Facebook: https://www.Facebook.com/carlosfederico.dejong
FB Art Page: https://www.Facebook.com/pages/
Carlos-de-Jong-Mixed-Media-Digital-Art/184212341720453

MARLENE JORGE - PAGES 32, 53

Marlene's art displays a complex set of influences from her rich and varied life. Born in the Dominican Republic, Marlene creates art that reflects her Caribbean inheritance with bold colors, stylized poses, echoes of the warm and tropical surroundings where the artist grew up. Intensely melancholic gazes and movement are essential elements to her oeuvre, as, too, is the gentle dominance of the human figure expressed in a nostalgic manner. One of the recurring features in Marlene's artwork is the accentuation of the figure through blank outlines in each one of her pieces dramatizing it in a illustrative way. Marlene has exhibited in over 30 art shows and galleries around the world. The artist now divides her time between New York and Austin,TX.

Visit her website at www.marlenejorge.com or contact her by phone at 512.903.7656 or by email at Jorgemarleneartist@gmail.com http://bookcollaborative.com/wp-content/uploads/2013/09/ Marlene-Jorge-p31.

KIMBERLY LAVELLE - PAGES 83, 85

Kimberly is an award-winning artist who has been exposed to fine art since childhood. She studied art at St. Edward's University in Austin, Texas. The majority of her work has been commissioned animal portraits and raptor paintings. Her intent with all of her portrait work is to capture and honor each individual personality and shows the spirit that she sees shining out through their eyes. Kimberly works with the Fort Collins Cat Rescue and Rocky Mountain Raptor Program donating works for their annual fundraisers and donating 25% of all commissioned work associated with their organizations back to them. View her work and contact her at www.fromtheheartwatercolors.com or on her Facebook page Kimberly Lavelle Watercolors.

NINH LE - PAGES 67, 109

Ninh Le lives in the city of Dien Bien Phu, Vietnam. He is a junior high school teacher there. He find inspiration in the gentle and romantic struggle of the ethnic people of the Vietnam highlands. Contact him by email at ninhledienbien@gmail.com or by phone at 0914 323 067. His Facebook page is Oil painting Ninh Le.

JACKIE SPECTOR LINDER - PAGE 74

Jackie has been a mosaic artist since 1999, when she decided to turn a lifelong passion for Mosaics into a full-time occupation. She is a recent transplant to Northern Westchester, New York, where she is a member of the Katonah Museum Artists Association.

It is Jackie's belief that mosaic art is an opportunity to recycle and reuse items that would otherwise be discarded. In a puzzle-like fashion, Jackie's artistic process begins with one small piece of stained glass, china or ceramic tile. Her portfolio includes but is not limited to mirrors, tables, frames and clocks. Jackie can be reached either through her website jackiespectorlinder.weebly.com or on her Facebook page Jackie Spector Linder mosaic artist.

LORALAI (LORYIA BOND) - PAGES 80, 95

Loralai lives in Columbus, Ohio, and is a lifelong art lover. Her Blue Cat Series is inspired by a rescue cat named Blue. Loralai is actively involved in promoting foster care and adoption of cats in need. She regularly donates a portion of the proceeds from her art sales to these worthy causes. See more of her artwork at:
www.Facebook.com/loralaioriginalart,
www.etsy.com/shop/mermaidartbyloralai,
www.fairyartbyloralai.blogspot.com.
Contact her about her artwork at admin@loralai.com,
loryia.bond@gmail.com, and by phone at 614-5610-344.

CHRISTINE MARSHALL - PAGES 68, 107

Christine is a UK artist who now lives and works in Boston. Her creative works include mixed media, abstract painting, and fine art photography. You can find her artwork and photography on the following websites.
FOR SALE on ETSY - www.etsy.com/shop/Key2MyArt
Follow me on Pinterest - www.pinterest.com/Key2MyArtStudio
Follow me on Facebook - www.Facebook.com/Key2MyArt
Follow me on Instagram - instagram.com/key2myartstudio
Follow me on TWITTER - twitter.com/Key2MyArt

AYUSH MEHRA - PAGES 84, 86

Ayush lives in the small city of Noida in India. He was born in 1997 and started painting in the first grade. By ninth grade he decided to make painting his life's work. With the support of his family, especially his father, he on his way to becoming an accomplished artist.

His Facebook Page is Portrait art by ayush or email him at mehra.ayushnew97@gmail.com.

YALILY MEJIA - PAGE 37

Dominican mosaic artist Yalily has been working with glass for more that 14 years. She began working with stained glass in her early teens.

She is a self-taught mosaic artist who likes to experiment with different styles and materials. Everything inspires; from nature, to art, to human behavior, to music, and even a fragrance can lead her to explore new things. Her main material is stained glass, but stone, smalti, ceramics, wood, and all kinds of things can be used for mosaics.

View her work and contact her on Facebook at:
http://www.facebook.com/yalilymejiamosaics

JEFF MONTAGNE - PAGE 81

Jeff is a wildlife artist from Sacramento, CA. He has been featuring wildlife in his artwork for over 13 years and has won numerous art awards. His deep respect for wildlife helps create his passion for his work. View his artwork on his Facebook page "Wildlife Art by Jeff Montagne" or at www.wildlifeartbyjm.com.
wildlifeartbyjm@gmail.com
jmart@wildlifeartbyjm.com

JIMMY ALEJANDRO GONZALES MORALES - PAGES 26, 110

Jimmy is a Guatemalan artist who teaches art and art history. He has exhibited in the Gallery Gran Hotel, Cronopios y Famas lounge and is a winner of the call for Gran Hotel 2014.

View his work on Facebook: https://www.Facebook.com/ArtCollageJimmy or Tumblr: http://cool-thejimz.tumblr.com/ Email: weed123gon@gmail.com

AIDA NOVOSEL - PAGES 24, 47, 91

Aida is a painter, fashion designer, costume designer, and set designer. She has received numerous awards for her work. Aida is a member of the Association of Fine Artists of Serbia. She has exhibited her work in Belgrade, Montenegro, Manhattan, Chicago, Toronto, and many other cities.

Visit her on Facebook at
https://www.Facebook.com/novosel.aida?fref=ts
or contact her at aidanovosel@gmail.com.

JOSEPH PALOTAS - PAGES 10, 28, 100

Joe is an experienced commission artist and works in many media. He infuses wild expressions of color to a wide variety of subject matter from portraits to abstracts to contemporary and mixed media landscapes. His works reflect a variety of creative styles. See more of Joe's work at his Facebook page Art In Wonderland or on his website, http://www.artsinwonderland.com.

ANGELIKA PARKER - PAGE 54

Angelika is the creative mind behind Art Love Passion. She loves to draw, paint and to create new designs on her computer. She has many different styles and talents. Her range goes from quirky illustrations, abstract digital art, as well as unique paintings to beautiful photography. You can find her paintings, painted vases and candle holders in her Etsy shop. Society6 as well as Redbubble prints her artwork and designs on various items, such as shirts, phone cases, pillow cases, art prints, duvet covers, clocks and many more. If this has sparked your interest, check out her art at: www.artlovepassion.com

VHILO PERSSON - PAGES 9, 57

Vhilo was born in 1972 in Sweden. He is a self-taught artist. His dedication to his artwork has helped him overcome many hardships in life. These include a homeless period and three bouts with cancer. In his words "My Art Saved My Life And If I Don't Paint I Die. It Is That Simple."

His work has exhibited in Sweden, United States, and Brussels. He is represented by a gallery in New York and his art will be in art fairs this year around the world. View his work at: www.vhilo-artist1.se. Contact him at: www.vhilo-artist1.se

BEATA PISKA - PAGES 17, 101

Beata was born in 1988, in Krynica Zdroj, Poland. He now lives in the small village of Lekawica in the south of Poland. He began painting at the age of 15 and now it is his biggest passion and hobby.

Visit his Facebook page: Beata Piska – Oil Painting
His website: http://beatapiskaoilpainting.wordpress.com/
Or on YouTube: www.youtube.com/user/beatapiska

ELEONORA PULCINI - PAGES 72, 104

Eleonora has always had a great passion for science and numbers. She studied civil engineering in Rome, Italy, and then moved to Melbourne, Australia. A big adventure that has inspired her new life and led into finding a new way to communicate with the world: ART. Her paintings are about this adventure, are about the dramatic battle of life, lights, nostalgia and hope. Family is her biggest value and getting you lost in endless perspective views is her biggest goal.

View her work at:
www.eleonorapulcini.wix.com/eleonorapulcini
www.Facebook.com/eleonora.oilpaintings
Email her at ep.mel2012@gmail.com

LESLIE RODRIGUEZ - PAGES 27, 41, 42

Leslie is a mixed media artist, she creates with just about anything, and her favorite medium is acrylic paint. She uses plaster, wood, fibers and paper in her art. Leslie tends to like dark colors and neutrals, but for some reason always end up with vibrant and loud colors in her art. She just goes with the flow, and she lets her imagination fly. She is currently pursuing her degree in graphic arts and has an Etsy shop. She is the mother to three teenage boys.

View her work at:
www.lelasworld.com and www.Facebook.com/lelart
Contact her at: 312-342-4602 or lesliemro@gmail.com

JILL RYALS - PAGES 15, 76

Jill is a self-taught artist from Oskaloosa, Iowa. She has been living in central Florida now most of her life and enjoying her garden and pets while keeping busy with a variety of original artworks.

Contact her at: Phone# 407-493-4745
Email jill_ryals@yahoo.com
Facebook at Jill Ryals Oil paintings and creative art

PAUL SADOWSKI - PAGES 35, 61, 62

Paul was born in 1981 in Bialystok, Poland. Since 2005, he has worked exclusively with painting and computer graphics. He studied architecture and urban planning in Bialystok University of Technology. The subject of his paintings is quite broad, from portraits and acts, through landscape and architecture, to emotional

and expressive images emanating reflection and symbolism.

Contact him at:
www.pawelsadowski.com
www.Facebook.com/paulsadowski.paintings
shadowskipawel@gmail.com

MITZI SATO-WIUFF - PAGE 82

Mitzi is a relative newcomer to the world of fantasy art, although she has been making art for a long time. Her distinct images are created by combining traditionally rendered line art in pen on paper with her unique digital coloring technique, using Corel Painter program, resulting in a look similar to works done in watercolor. When she's not painting fantasy images, she enjoys teaching Japanese to American students, playing the piano, taking care of her goldfish and freshwater tropical fish tanks, playing with her family cats, gardening, cooking, and reading. View her work at www.auroawings.com or on her Facebook page "Fantasy Art of Mitzi." Contact her at studiomiyabi@aol.com.

CAROLYN SCHLAM - PAGES 16, 30, 48, 92

Carolyn is a painter, mixed media and glass artist living and working in Taos, New Mexico. She is also an illustrator of children's books and the author of *The Creative Path: Process and Practice.* Her work can be seen on her website at www.carolynschlam.com and purchased directly or through the galleries that represent her work. Her work can be purchased also online through www.artquiver.com. Contact Carolyn through her website, her email at carolynschlam@aol.com, or by phone at 786-897-2276. She accepts commissions in all media.

ELLEN SCHLOBOHM - PAGES 49, 106

Ellen is a South Australian-based artist who has been working

in paper for the last five years. Ellen started papercutting in high school where she was inspired by a beautiful book called *This is for you* by UK papercut artist Rob Ryan. From there Ellen continued to develop her practice, having several exhibitions, creating commissioned work and exploring a variety of artistic avenues. Ellen's work is created by meticulously cutting away paper to leave behind delicate tableaus. It is often whimsical in nature with the inclusion of text to give it a contemporary slant. Ellen is drawn to paper as a medium for its simplicity and delicate nature and loves to watch this humble material come alive as each cut is made and the image revealed.

Contact her at:
Website: http://www.ellenmarieartistry.com/
Facebook: https://Facebook.com/ellenmarieartistry
Twitter: http://twitter.com/emsartistry
Instagram: http://instagram.com/ellenmarieartistry

PATRICIA ELLIOTT SEITZ - PAGES 69, 109

Patricia was born in San Diego, California, and spent most of her young adulthood living in Southern California. She came from a background of art and music, and always knew that she wanted to be an artist. Her love for landscapes and seascapes has been heavily influenced by where she has lived through the years. Her painting approach is based on Impressionism, and Tonalism. Her main subject matter is landscapes and seascapes. Today she can be found in her studio, painting seasonal paintings of the Central New York area and the California coastlines. She is an active member of Oil Painters of America and CNY Art Guild, and her work is represented by local NY art Galleries. See more of her work at www.patriciaseitz.com.

GOLNAZ SHOBEIRI - PAGE 34

Golnaz is a Persian artist and the only known artist in the United States who employs the vitray method of glass painting that she learned from the masters. Golnaz studied for two years with master Persian artists Mr. Taeb and Iraj Javanshir.

Golnaz makes her own paste for the traditional vitray process and mixes her own colors. The results are the rich, deep colors associated with stained glass artists combined with the classic designs of Persian architecture that come alive in the paintings of Golnaz, who now lives in Woodland Hills, California.

Golnaz assembles a mixture of geometric shapes and colors onto glass and shares her thoughts and feelings in the same manner as the classic Persian artists. The results are stunning, colorful wall paintings and tabletops of precisely cut geometric shapes on glass. View her work at: golnazart.com, Facebook page Golnaz Shobeiri: Artist on Glass

FERENC SOMOGYI - PAGES 22,108

Ferenc is a sculptor from Hungary. He creates wooden reliefs of mystic colorful women. For him, the most beautiful things in life are women and trees. Both are so magical and vital. His work components are dainty humor, enchanting erotica, perfectly carved details and an interesting tale, with all these in proportion as they are in life. His Facebook page is Ferenc Somogyi Sculptor.
Website: http://somogyiszobrok.blogspot.com.
Email: somogyi.feri@gmail.com

JOEL TESCH - PAGES 18, 105

Joel is a San Francisco-based artist who produces acrylic and mixed media paintings in a variety of styles and subjects. His work is available for purchase, commissions, and public showings. He has exhibited in several locations on both coasts and is a frequent

exhibitor in juried fine art shows. Several pieces are now owned by private collectors all over the world.

Visit his Facebook page Joel Tesch Studio or his Etsy shop at: http://www.etsy.com/shop/JoelTeschGallery or his website: http://joeltesch.com/.

SAMANTHA THOMPSON - PAGES 39, 70

Samantha's pastel and acrylic paintings display a complex of influences from her rich and varied life. She was born in Sydney in 1978. Having worked and exhibited around the world including New York and London, her last major influence was living in the most Art Deco city in the universe, Napier in New Zealand. Samantha's paintings are a masterful blend of form, style and content, incorporating the rich habitat she has encountered during her short itinerant life. Visit her Facebook page Samantha Thompson—Artist or view her artwork at www.samanthathompson.com.au.

LUBOSH VALENTA - PAGES 52, 77

Lubosh is a Czech artist living in Prague. He started with art creation as late as in his thirties. His work was changing by years of self-study up to a present image. Oil painting soon became his favorite technique. He created hundreds of oil paintings in the last 20 years, most of them in surrealist style, and he had 16 exhibitions across the whole Czech Republic. In 2000, he contributed to the increase in promotion of amateur art in the Czech Republic by establishing the website "Amateur Picture gallery" which associated hundreds of Czech artists and exposed tens of thousands of paintings. Contact him at: website www.lubosh-obrazy.cz, Email: luboshv@centrum.cz Facebook Page: https://www.Facebook.com/lubosh.painting

CHRISTOPHER VIDAL - PAGES 102

Christopher is an artist residing in Sydney, Australia. His interest in art started from when he was very young. His artistic work varies from traditional landscapes in oils and acrylics to his latest experimental abstract work. His landscapes are inspired by nature which he paints in a realistic way using impressionistic techniques. In his paintings he always tries to capture the moment as light is reflected from mountains, clouds and ocean. The sounds of the ocean, winds and singing birds are his inspiration. Christopher is a member of a number of art societies and he exhibits regularly in local art shows and venues. His work can be viewed at www.christopher-vidal.com.au and other social media networks. He accepts commissioned work and can be reached at artist@christopher-vidal.com or info@vidalartsandphotography.com.au.

YEOK - PAGE 58

Yeok is a traditionally trained artist who lives and works in Melbourne, Australia. She learned how to draw and paint in an art institution in China throughout her childhood. Graduated from Monash University as a multimedia designer, Yeok was working as a commercial graphic/web designer and marketing consultant before she launched her art career in 2012. In November 2013, Yeok's debut solo show "In search of happiness" instantly gathered attention from local art enthusiasts. She continued her journey in Nov ember 2014 with her second solo exhibition "A walk on the dark side." It tells the story of her 12-months journey in the form of a surreal fantasy.

Contactherat:http://yeok.com.au,http://Facebook.com/yeokart, http://instagram.com/yeokart.

Index of Quotations

About the Author

BRADFORD G. WHELER is the former CEO, President and Co-owner of Allan Electric Company. He sold Allan Electric to a New York Stock Exchange listed company. After staying on as President during the transition, Brad retired.

Brad's lifelong love of history, art, books, and the inherent humor in man's nature led to the founding of BookCollaborative.com and the publishing of *Inca's Death Cave* as well as *GOLF SAYINGS: wit & wisdom of a good walk spoiled*, *CAT SAYINGS: wit & wisdom from the whiskered ones*, *HORSE SAYINGS: wit & wisdom straight from the horse's mouth*, *DOG SAYINGS: wit & wisdom from man's best friend*, and *SNAPPY SAYINGS: wit & wisdom from the world's greatest minds.*

His community involvements include being a Trustee of Community General Hospital in Hamilton, NY, and chairing their Finance Committee. He is the former Chairman of the Board of Trustees of Cazenovia College, and former Chairman and member of the Board of Directors and Alumni Association and President of the Sigma Phi Society at Cornell University in Ithaca, NY. He is also a former member of the Board of Directors of the Greater Cazenovia Area Chamber of Commerce and several other boards.

Brad played polo on the Cornell University men's polo team for four years and was a member of the Cazenovia Polo Club. In 2012 he was inducted into the Manlius Pebble Hill Athletic Hall of Fame.

He holds a BS and ME in Civil and Environmental Engineering from Cornell University in Ithaca, NY, as well as an MBA degree from Fordham University in New York, NY.

Brad, his wife, Julie, and their golden retriever Finlay live in Cazenovia, NY and Fort Pierce, FL.

Buy These Books at a Discount on www.BookCollaborative.com

They are also available on Amazon.com and Barnes&Noble.com. You can order them at any bookstore in the US, UK, and Canada for delivery within a few days.

All books available in eBook form on Amazon.com.

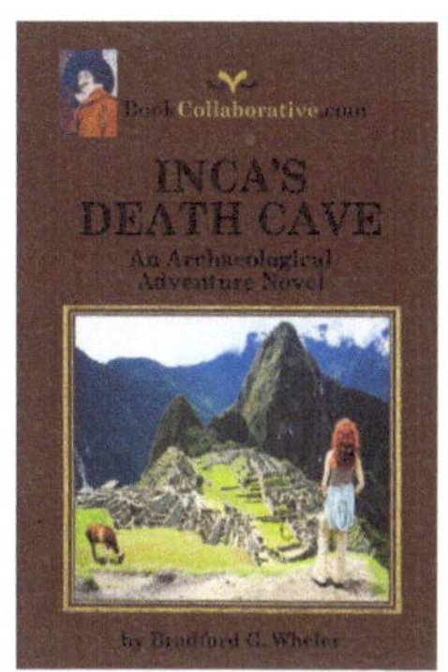

INCA'S DEATH CAVE An Archaeological Mystery Thriller

By Bradford G. Wheler

Twenty-one 5 Star reviews

Adventure, archaeology, technology, and mystery mix to form a breathtaking action-packed tale.

A 500-year-old puzzle catapults an archaeology professor and his brilliant grad student into the adventure of a lifetime in INCA'S DEATH CAVE, a new mystery thriller from author Bradford G. Wheler.

What happened to a band of Inca rebels who journeyed north in Peru to seek the fabled cave of the true gods – and escape the disease and destruction brought by Spanish conquistadors? They were never heard from again. Did they just melt back into their villages or was something more sinister involved? What trace or treasure did they leave behind?

The ingenious plot of this thriller is full of twists and turns, excitement and adventure, archaeology and technology. Readers will meet fascinating characters they'll never forget: a high-tech billionaire, a quick-witted professor, his beautiful young student, and her still-tough grandfather, a retired Marine gunny sergeant.

Cornell University professor Robert Johnson and his star PhD student are hired by a billionaire entrepreneur to solve a 500-year-old archaeology mystery in northern Peru. But first, they will have to survive corporate skullduggery and drug-lord thuggery. And why, 6,700 miles away in Vatican City, is the old guard so upset? What dark secrets could centuries-old manuscripts hold?

This assiduously researched, fast-paced novel brings the Incas and their ancestors to life against the backdrop of the Peruvian Andes.

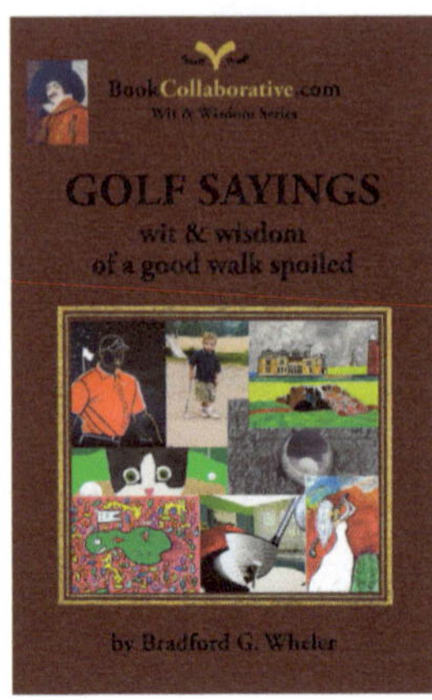

GOLF SAYINGS
wit & wisdom of a good walk spoiled

Seven 5 Star reviews

Lots and lots of wisdom on these pages and a lot of chuckles

By D. Blankenship, Amazon top 50 and Hall of Fame reviewer.

I have quite a few books whose subject matter deals exclusively with "golf sayings." I have been collecting these books since I first started playing some 55 odd years ago. Of all the wonderful reading I have on my shelf; all the wisdom, humor and frustration documented in their pages concerning what is probably the greatest game every invented, this little work is most certainly in the exclusive top five I own.

CAT SAYINGS
wit & wisdom from the whiskered ones

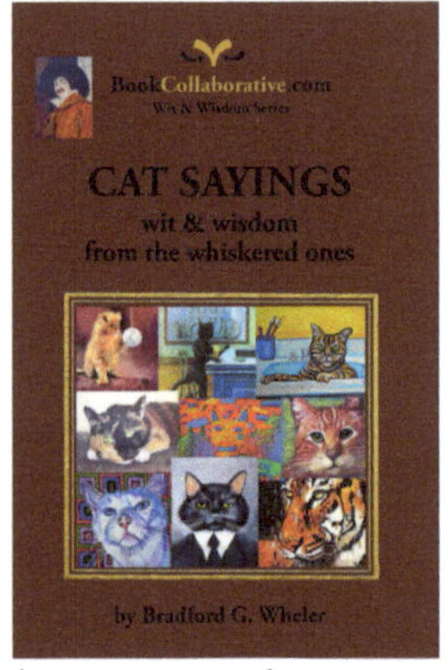

Thirteen 5 Star reviews

Feline Art and Words: For cat lovers and those who attempt to understand them

By Grady Harp, Amazon top 50 and Hall of Fame Reviewer

Brad G. Wheler has curated an art and words spectrum devoted to Cats (note the capital C and you'll get the gist of this book!). There is about as much variety of artwork reproduced on every page of this enormously entertaining book as is mirrored in the variety of excerpts of words from the ancients to the moderns. Wheler wisely keeps the reader's interest by dividing his book into chapters: Cats Rule, Wild Cats, Kittens, Humor, Of Cats and Dogs, The Cat Personality, Death of a Friend, Love Of, Cats Vs. People - each topic is generously illustrated with art and comments pertinent to each subsection.

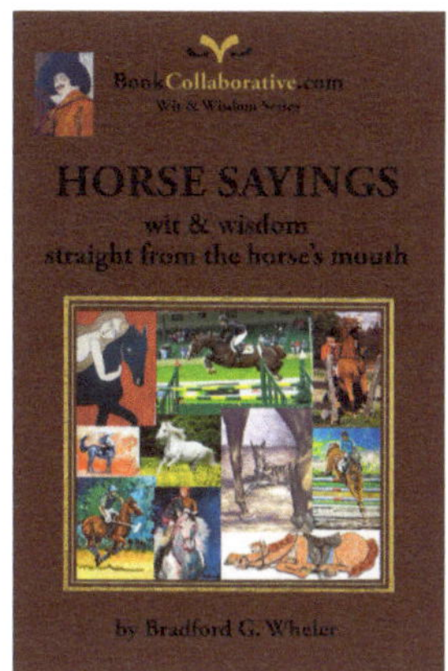

HORSE SAYINGS
wit & wisdom straight from the horse's mouth

Nine 5 Star reviews

Horse Enthusiasts Rejoice!

By Dr. Joseph S. Maresca, Amazon top 1000 and Hall of Fame reviewer

Horse Sayings; Wit and Wisdom Straight from the Horse's Mouth by Bradford G. Wheler depicts the horse in all of its glory together with the continued human interest in the equine. The presentation has pearls of wisdom from horse humor, competition, ancient wisdom, training and many other aspects of horses unbeknownst to the public generally but well known to horse enthusiasts. There are illustrations by 61 artists from 11 countries.

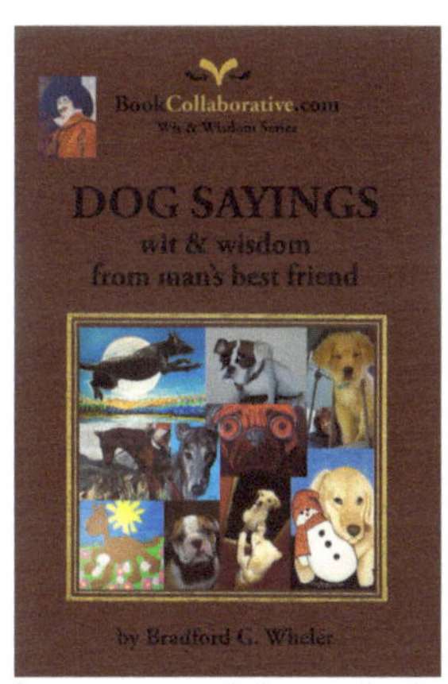

DOG SAYINGS
wit & wisdom from man's best friend

Three 5 Star reviews

A Choice Read, Solidly Recommended

By Midwest Book Review

The simple mutts can be far wiser than they let on. *Dog Sayings; Wit & Wisdom from Man's Best Friend* looks at a collection of humor and knowledge as well as plenty of art focusing on man's constant canine companion. For centuries, there has been much said about the relationship of man and dog, and much inspiration has been drawn from them. Presented in full color throughout, *Dog Sayings* is a choice read, solidly recommended.

SNAPPY SAYINGS
wit & wisdom from the world's greatest minds

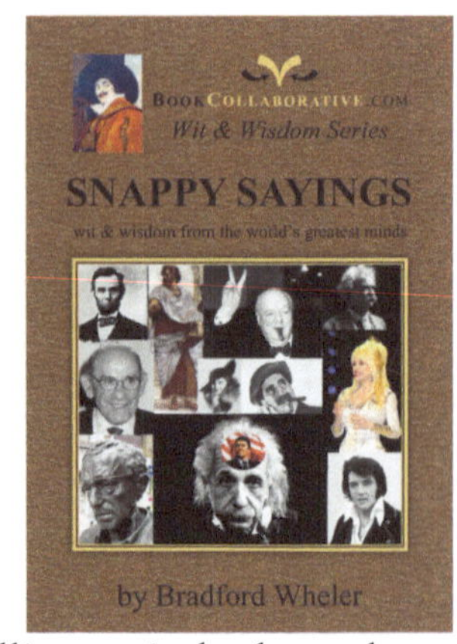

Nine 5 Star reviews

A Top Pick for Anyone Looking for a Solid Collection of Humor

By Midwest Book Review

The best wit and wisdom comes from the best minds. Snappy Sayings is a compilation of quips from countless brilliant minds throughout history, from hundreds of years ago to the modern day. Divided into the many aspects of human nature and the unique quips delivered from these individuals, *Snappy Sayings* is a collection that will lead to hours of entertainment. *Snappy Sayings* is a top pick for anyone looking for a solid collection of humor.

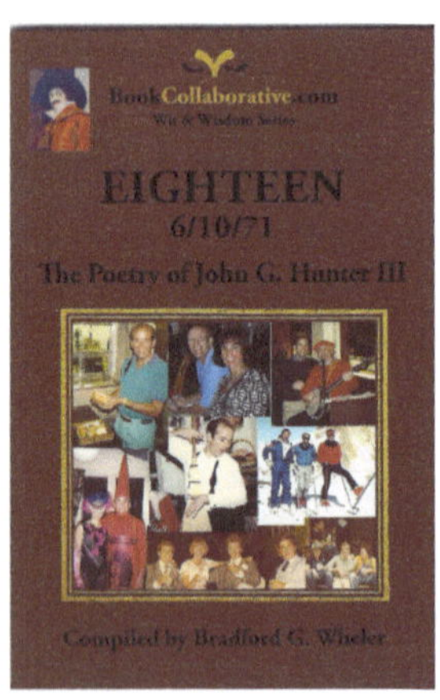

EIGHTEEN 6/10/71
The Poetry of John G. Hunter III

is a collection of poems written by John G. Hunter III and given to Bradford G. Wheler for his eighteenth birthday on June 10, 1971. Each poem is accompanied by a color photograph. The layout and design was done by the renowned Italian book designer Adira Cucicov. Wheler has said many times, "I'm sure I received many fine gifts on my 18th birthday but this is the only one I remember and still treasure."

www.ingramcontent.com/pod-product-compliance
Lightning Source LLC
LaVergne TN
LVHW052251100826
845147LV00001B/20

* 9 7 8 0 9 8 2 2 5 3 8 8 5 *